NO EASY WALK

The Dramatic Journey of African-Americans

HARRY LOUIS WILLIAMS II

InterVarsity Press
Downers Grove, Illinois

Dedicated to the memory of my mother,
the late Claudette Maudine Davis Williams,
the godliest person whom I have ever known,
and my uncle, Samuel Williams,
who gave me the opportunity to reroute my destiny.

InterVarsity Press
P.O. Box 1400, Downers Grove, IL 60515
World Wide Web: www.ivpress.com
E-mail: mail@ivpress.com

©1998 by Harry Louis Williams II

InterVarsity Press® is the book-publishing division of InterVarsity Christian Fellowship/USA®, a student movement active on campus at hundreds of universities, colleges and schools of nursing in the United States of America, and a member movement of the International Fellowship of Evangelical Students. For information about local and regional activities, write Public Relations Dept., InterVarsity Christian Fellowship/USA, 6400 Schroeder Rd., P.O. Box 7895, Madison, WI 53707-7895.

All Scripture quotations, unless otherwise indicated, are taken from the Holy Bible, New International Version®. NIV®. Copyright ©1973, 1978, 1984 by International Bible Society. Used by permission of Zondervan Publishing House. All rights reserved.

Cover: Wooden carving after Dogon style African art, SuperStock; Three Freedom Fighters, Anna Belle Lee Washington/Superstock

ISBN 0-8308-1792-1

Printed in the United States of America ♾

Library of Congress Cataloging-in-Publication Data

Williams, Harry Louis.
  No easy walk: the dramatic journey of African-Americans/Harry
Louis Williams II.
       p.   cm.
    Includes bibliographical references (p.   ).
    ISBN 0-8308-1792-1 (pbk.: alk. paper)
    1. Afro-Americans—History.   2. Afro-Americans—Religion.
I. Title.
E185.W75   1999
973'.0496073—dc21   *98-31012*
                                                                          CIP

| 19 | 18 | 17 | 16 | 15 | 14 | 13 | 12 | 11 | 10 | 9 | 8 | 7 | 6 | 5 | 4 | 3 | 2 | 1 |

| 13 | 12 | 11 | 10 | 09 | 08 | 07 | 06 | 05 | 04 | 03 | 02 | 01 | 00 | 99 | 98 |

contents

Prologue

· ·

Whispers of Blackness

I am a black man. I live on the dangling precipice of the late twentieth century and the early edge of the twenty-first. And I am more than what you see.

I am fertile gardens and barren deserts, plush palaces of the past and public housing projects of the present. I am kings and kingpins. I am heroes and hit men. I am Marcus Garvey, Medgar Evers, Harriet Tubman, Malcolm X and Huey P. Newton. I am open doors and higher visions. I am the hopes and the laughter and the prayers and the tears of my people through the centuries.

I am more than what you see. I am history. I am the heir of a fortune richer than melanin. In my heart I hold the chronicles of my people, the stories of our world passed down from generation to generation. The dreams of my ancestors flow through my bloodstream. I am more than what you see.

Once, in my imagination, I walked across the portals of history. I did not land in the tropical paradise of the Caribbean. I did not open my mind's eye in Chile or Spain or Senegal. In my imagination I landed on the M15 bus in Manhattan, New York City.

The huge vehicle headed past the midtown area. Soon we were

rolling past some of the richest real estate in the world, Central Park West. Immaculately dressed doormen smiled thinly from in front of their luxury high-rises—architectural marvels most of them.

And then the bus careened across West 110th Street. We were in Harlem. Some call West 110th the invisible wall. The combined aromas of fried plantains and burnt car tires welcomed me to Third World America. This is where America hides its poor.

I walked past the crumbling shells of fire-gutted tenements. Broken glass littered broken sidewalks. A collage of churches, medical centers, fast-food joints and pinball parlors lined the streets. The Chinese take-out restaurant had a bulletproof glass partition. I stopped in a candy store that sold chewing gum and crack pipes. The radio blared Curtis Mayfield's old song, "If There's Hell Below (We're All Gonna Go)."

Finally I found him. There he was, standing in the doorway of a rust-colored five-story walk-up on Lenox Avenue. His eyes flitted nervously from one bustling corner to another. He wore a navy blue woolen cap pulled down over his nest of gray hair. His green army fatigue jacket drooped down over the shoulders of his near skeletal frame. His gray-and-white beard needed trimming.

He skipped the formalities. "Boy, ain't you s'posed to be in school or something? What you doing up here?"

I said, "Great-great-great-great Grandpa, I want you to tell me something that they won't tell me in school."

"And what might that be, son?" the old man asked.

"Tell me your story, Grandpa. Tell me where you come from—where we come from."

In my imagination, I lost myself in Grandpa's oratory, and he began to wander around in my mind. This is what he said.

Once I clenched my teeth in the odorous bowels of a slave ship bound for a place I did not know. I found myself trembling in airless darkness amidst the sounds of moaning and crying from my fellow captives. I was entombed in a space smaller than a coffin.

The wooden floorboards ripped the flesh from my naked back as the ship bucked and rolled with each wave of the open sea. There were neither windows nor adequate waste facilities down below. The stench was horrific. After a few weeks, all cries for mercy died in my heart and throat.

Although there were hundreds of us huddled in that crowded ship's compartment, my tears alone gave me companionship. We were all of different nations, and few spoke the same tongue.

Heaven dropped a single particle of relief on my parched soul in the predawn hours of the morning. It was offered by a lowly seaman who kept watch on the upper decks during the night watch. The sweet sound of his golden tenor voice would filter through the floorboards to the hell beneath his feet. Night after night he would sing, "Oh, How Sweet the Name of Jesus." *Who is Jesus?* I would wonder as I fell into a fitful sleep.

Three months later, I found myself chained to an auction block deep in the southern heart of someplace called America. I was as naked as Adam and just as ashamed.

A white man I had never seen before poked and prodded me with a stick. I was confused, more confused than I'd ever been in my life. He exchanged money for the possession of my being that day. I was dumped into a wagon, shackled to it and transported to a tobacco plantation. As I breathed in the fresh pine scent of Virginia air, I denied myself forever the hope that I would see my loved ones in Africa again.

Master was a good man, according to my fellow field hands. He would wield the bullwhip only when an errant slave deserved it. Too often, I found myself errant.

We worked Master's fields from sunup to sundown. Religious gentleman that he was, he allowed us to take Sundays off. The practice was derived from the Ten Commandments. He would often quote, "Remember the Sabbath day to keep it holy."

On Sundays, Master and his wife required their slaves to accompany them to the beautiful brown brick church in town. It was here that my relationship with Master took on a bit of a twist. You see, Master was the pastor of the church. Therefore, he was also my pastor.

Upon entering the church edifice, my fellow bondsmen and I would trudge up the back stairs to the Negro gallery. It was a balcony suspended high above the rear of the sanctuary. From our perch in the segregated section, we could maintain a perfect overhead view of the church service below.

The worshipers below us dressed in the most fashionable of formalwear. My fellow slaves and I dressed in rags. Some of us were barefoot.

Master was a fine preacher. However, it was the music that I loved most about the church. Often while laboring in the field I would secretly fantasize about what it might be like to stand with the choir and lend my baritone to the hymns. Alas, all that it would ever be was a dream.

During my first Sunday morning in church, I made a spectacle of myself. I'm still ashamed when I think about it. It happened during the opening hymn. As the choir and the piano came together in magnificent harmony, I recognized the tune. They were singing, "Oh, How Sweet the Name of Jesus."

With hot, involuntary tears running down my cheeks I leaned over and asked the slave woman next to me, "Who is Jesus?"

She just shrugged her shoulders, puzzled by my sobbing.

One day old Master called the slaves to the big house on the plantation. With tears in his eyes he read from a long scroll called the Emancipation Proclamation. I didn't understand much of what he was reading until he pronounced the word "freedom." I had my bags packed and had hit the front gate before he got to Abraham Lincoln's signature.

Although I had worked for Master for years, he released me without so much as a new set of underwear. I didn't care. I was just glad the whippings had stopped.

Things went well for me. I married a good woman and we raised a family on a nearby plantation. I was what folks called a sharecropper. I leased a parcel of property from a southern gentlemen. I was obligated to give him a generous share of the land's yieldings in exchange for its use. I often ended up owing more than the harvest brought in.

I was just settling into things when my eldest son came running home with some bad news. He'd sassed a white man in town. I'd tried my best to instill in him the Southern way, but he was still a slow learner. Back then slow learners lived short lives.

That night the scent of fear awoke me from a deep sleep. In the distance I could hear the beating of horse hoofs falling like approaching thunder. I levitated out of bed and went to the front window. What I saw made my heart pump like a jackhammer.

Men dressed like ghosts rode back and forth in front of the house. Their faces were secreted behind white linen masks with pointed caps. Shotguns peeked out from beneath their long white robes. A few of the horsemen carried torches. There were ten of them in all.

Two of the ghosts struggled with a big, heavy item which they'd toted in the back of a horse-drawn cart. It was a wooden cross. The first man seemed to stumble beneath its weight. A second man came to his aid, and they brought it to rest not fifteen feet from our front door. They worked silently. The only sound to be heard was the singing of the crickets.

I looked around me. My wife and children were gathered around me in the darkness, clinging tightly to my garments. They were awash in tears, too terrified to speak. I was helpless. We watched hypnotized as the men set the cross upright and planted it in the ground in front of the door. The scent of kerosene filled the air. And then in an instant the cross went up in flames. In the eerie glow of the burning cross I saw the eyes of Satan. His were cold, expressionless eyes that peered at me through the holes in a specter's mask.

The men rode away in complete silence. All was still except for the crackling of the wood and the crickets. Then, as the parade reached the road beyond my house, I heard singing. It was the lone voice of a church deacon that I knew. He was singing the unmistakable melody, "Oh, How Sweet the Name of Jesus."

I was dumbfounded. I pulled my family close to me and looked up toward the ceiling. "Who is Jesus?" I asked out loud. No one answered.

The next day I packed up my family and headed for New York City, New York. We landed in Harlem. We moved into a tenement walk-up across the street from a church named Deliverance.

My wife has gone on now. My children have moved away. But I am still here. Like the waters of the Niger River, my times have continuously flowed. Like the all-seeing eyes of the Sphinx back in ancient Egypt, still I gaze into the sunset on lush summer evenings. Like time itself, my days are endless. Yet I have never been inside of Deliverance.

On warm summer nights I like to sit on the front stoop of my building and tap my feet to the singing of the choir. Sometimes I wonder how they can sing over all the hell being raised out here. I wonder how the sopranos can chirp over the sounds of gunshots. I wonder how the baritones can resonate amidst the dense droning of police sirens. Yet it happens, night after night.

One night last week as I sat on the stoop, service began inside of the sanctuary of Deliverance. The sounds of the organ and piano belting out all of my favorite hymns had my hands clapping. The choir sang "How I

Got Over" and then faded into "Oh, How Sweet the Name of Jesus."

Emotion overcame me as the melody filled the streets. I found myself fighting back memories which came floating out of my eyes disguised as tears. *Who is Jesus?* Again, I wondered.

I had heard stories of a man by that name who fed five thousand people with a little boy's lunch. And yet these church people do nothing to help the suffering of the poor, the hungry and the aged but sing to them. They call the church Deliverance, but they never helped one of these neighborhood children get a college scholarship. They never set up a daycare center for working mothers.

I would think to myself, *There are Third World countries where people live longer on average than in Harlem, how they speaking on that at Deliverance? And these drugs! If somebody came here as a tourist, they'd think drugs was legal in this neighborhood. What are they doing about it? I been to the Board of Education meeting begging these people to do something about these broken-down schools we sending our kids too. How come that preacher from Deliverance never goes to the meetings?*

Sometimes I just shake my head and say, "Deliverance from what?"

Back on the plantation, I'd heard a story I liked—they say Jesus told it. It was about this man who found somebody beat up by the side of the road. He didn't start testifying or singing. He fixed the man's wounds, tied him up with bandages and then took him to a hotel to heal up. He even paid his room and board till he got better. To me, living in this place of madness, *that* sounded like deliverance.

I kept thinking about God and justice and love. *You can't split no man in half and just save his soul for heaven while the rest of him lives in hell on earth! I mean, there's two worlds in New York, one poor and one nice, one black and one white. They tell me those Old Testament prophets like Amos and Isaiah used to kick up dust 'bout that sort of thing. If you call yourself delivering somebody then you got to talk about racism and you got to talk to it wherever you find it. Real religion is going to save all the person, not just the soul.*

They'll never get nobody like me to go to Deliverance because they don't know my story, I mumbled to myself that night. *How can you save somebody's life and you don't know what they dying of? How can you look at me and say, "I love you," and you ain't took time to listen to me or get to know me. Man,* I thought, *somebody should tell them my story.*

They don't even know who I am.

A blast interrupted my meditations. I guessed it to be a .357 magnum or some other heavy-gauge firearm. Its thunder rang out again. People began to scatter through the streets. Some dove for cover. The old saying goes, "Bullets don't have no name on them." As old as I am, I ran through the front door of the building like Superman with his cape on fire.

I closed the blinds and turned off all the lights and then I laid on the floor real still. That's what they told me to do "when the shootin' and carrying-on starts to commencin'." And there in the stillness it came to me, and I got the chills.

I'm an old man but I have a story. No, I *am* the story. Hundreds and hundreds of years of history penetrate my soul. I have been both a warrior and a slave, a patriot and a pyramid builder, the conquered and the conqueror, a kingpin and a wise man. My tale is told with the ragged holler of a long-silenced voice from deep within a palace dungeon. I thought to myself, *I'm going to write my story down and send it to the church across the street. I want them to know who I am.*

I gathered myself up off of the floor and pulled up to my little wooden desk. I found two or three pieces of blue and white notebook paper and a black pen that said "Hotel Theresa" on it in gold leaf.

I started to write down the names of my family members as they came to me. Ham. Martin Luther King. Sojourner Truth. Shaka Zulu. Arthur Ashe. Soon I could hear the pacing of their feet as they joined me in the room. I could hear the dragging of a slave's thick iron chains across the black linoleum tiles on my floor. I shivered at the shrill of a mighty Ashanti war cry. I could hear old songs—slave songs about Pharaoh, redemption and deliverance.

And I could hear my people speaking, whispering to me there in that cold-water flat in Harlem. They were whispering their lives to me. That night I heard whispers of blackness. And I wrote down what I could.

Part One

. . . .

West Africa
in Antiquity

*I*n Spike Lee's 1992 film *Malcolm X*, the incarcerated Muslim leader confronts his Christian past during a weekly prison chapel service. The worship facility is sparsely populated with inmates. Boredom has done her evil work during the Christian clergyman's exercise in homiletics. Prisoners stare dispassionately into space. Daydreams of better times twinkle in their eyes.

Suddenly Malcolm breaks the preacher's monologue with a question. The preacher is caught off guard; his white cheeks turn crimson. The other prisoners suddenly come back to life. Mumbling fills the awkward silence between question and response. Malcolm's words hang in space. "[Then] you can't believe for certain that Jesus was white?"

The clergyman finally replies in his finest New England accent, God is white. Isn't that obvious?"

Yes, it would be obvious if one were to examine the portraits of Christ painted over the past millennium. Jesus and all other biblical figures are usually portrayed as Europeans. Even the angels are blond and blue-eyed. Only the devil is traditionally portrayed as being red or black.

History's mischief does not stop there. For centuries books—and then movies—have portrayed the African as a savage who swung from trees in the jungle. Tarzan was introduced as a correct representation of the African people—moronic creatures who practically walked on their knuckles. Was it true? Were these the people that the early European traders found when they arrived on the West African coast in the fifteenth century?

In part one we will examine the biblical records of African people. We will also discover ancient West Africa, the home of the African-American's ancestors.

1

....

The Ancient
Patriarch

*H*am fell prostrate on the cold, damp ground. His stubby, calloused fingers clutched at the wet clumps of grass beneath his hands. His thick lips kissed the blackness of the earth.

Tears of joy and sadness left the corners of his eyes and intermingled at his chin. There was much reason for joy. Ham was ecstatic at the sight of a new day's dawning glory. He shivered involuntarily at the sound of birds chirping free in the distance. He stared incredulously at the clouds as they rolled around the heavens. For the first time in months, he allowed himself the luxury of a smile.

And yet Ham's heart was heavy. The screams of his neighbors and childhood friends still echoed in his head. He could hear the drumming of wet hands beating on the door of the wooden ark—their cries of "Let us in, let us in!" drowned out eventually by the torrential rains (Gen 7:16).

Ham and his wife and sons paced listlessly around the base of the ark. True, they were on land now. But trauma had etched its bitter lines on their faces. For months they'd been imprisoned in a floating zoo along with thousands of God's screeching, roaring beasts. Upon disembarking from the ark, they found themselves alone in a quiet place of desolation called Mount Ararat (Gen 8:4). The world they had once known was gone.

The First Black Man

It is a shame that the original parchments of the Bible did not contain multicolor illustrations. For if artists had been conscripted to draw portraits of biblical figures, some of the great theological debates would never have existed. The evil particularities of ethnocentrism would not have been able to color every biblical character of noteworthy virtue as a white person. Perhaps such ancient artists would have captured the full spectrum of God's human rainbow. In any case, there would be faded representative renderings of all of God's people in his book. There would be people like Ham.

Ham. Was he light-complexioned? Did his skin have a deep, rich, almost black tan? Was he short, or was he tall? Was his nose broad? Did he have thick lips? There are no pictures, no oral descriptions to shed light on these questions. What we do know is that Ham is the father of African humanity. The name *Ham* can be translated as "darkened," "dark brown" or "black." It can also means "warm," "hot" or "to be or become warm."[1]

The Hebrew Scriptures list Ham's progeny in a well-notated table of nations (Gen 10). The ancient chroniclers state that Ham's son Mizraim settled the lands of Egypt. Egypt appears under the synonym *Mizraim* on four separate occasions in the Old Testament. Some believe that it was recorded thus to connect it to Noah's son, Ham. The Bible also refers to Egypt as "the land of Ham."

According to historian John G. Jackson, the ancient residents of Egypt called their country "Khem," "Kam" or "Ham." He claims that this would be translated as "the black land." Jackson goes on to say that the Egyptians referred to themselves as "Khem, Kamites or Hamites (the black people.)"[2]

A famed Senegalese Egyptologist, the late Cheikh Ante Diop, proclaimed, "The Egyptians had only one term to designate themselves, =*Kmt*= (literally, 'the Negroes'). This is the strongest existing term to indicate blackness."[3] Diop stakes his claim on the veracity of the biblical chroniclers. He claims that the ancient Semitic traditionalists classified Egypt with the black countries. "The importance of these depositions can not be ignored," Diop writes, ". . . for these peoples (the Jews) which lived side by side with the ancient Egyptians and sometimes in symbiosis with them had nothing to gain by presenting a false ethnic picture of them."[4]

For centuries European-based scholarship has severed any historical connection between Egypt and the rest of the continent on which it stands. Many museums offer two separate viewing areas for Egypt and Africa. This in itself is ironic, since any world map proves that the two are actually one.

The media has participated in a form of racial bias for many years. One classic example is found in Cecil B. De Mille's epic motion picture *The Ten Commandments*. The film starred Elizabeth Taylor as Pharaoh Rameses's wife. A cast of thousands was recruited to portray the ancient Egyptians. Few of them showed up on the set with as much as a suntan. Were the Egyptians white people? The debate concerning their ethnicity continues even today.

European author Basil Davidson has written extensively on the subject of African history and sociology. He said, "Unlike Europeans of our times, the great historians of Greece had no conception of Egypt's not being a part of Africa; they would have thought such an idea absurd. Ancient Egypt largely was the Africa they knew and respected."[5]

Speculation exists about the origin of the early Egyptians. Some scholars hold to the belief that settlers from the African interior originally populated the country. Diordorus of Sicily wrote a history of the world in 50 B.C. He stated, "Now the Ethiopians [i.e., black peoples], as historians relate, were the first of all men, and the proofs of this statement are manifest." He later wrote, "The Egyptians were colonists sent out by the Ethiopians."[6]

In the fifth century B.C. Herodotus, a Greek historian from Asia Minor, traveled through Egypt. His eyewitness accounts claimed that the Egyptians had "black skins" and "wooly hair."[7]

In A.D. 1787 French explorer Count Volney visited Egypt. He was amazed at what he found. He said this:

> To think that a race of black men who today are our slaves and the object of our contempt is the same one to whom we owe our arts, sciences and even the use of our speech. . . . [T]here is a people now forgotten who discovered, while others were yet barbarians, the element of arts and sciences. A race of men now rejected from society for their sable skin and wooly hair whose civil and religious systems still govern the universe.[8]

Cush

Cush was a huge tract of real estate. Its borders were said to have spanned from India to West Africa and as far south as ancient Ghana.[9] This was the region that is present-day Mauritania. In the ancient world Cush was famous for its rich gold and precious mineral deposits. The Greeks called the country "Ethiopia," which was translated "land of the burnt faces." The Arabs coined the phrase "Bilad as Sudan" or "land of the blacks." The Egyptians called it "the Southern lands." The Hebrew people knew it as "Cush" (often spelled "Kush").

Cushites made ships from bulrushes. They exported ebony, elephants, jewelry and iron products. They held extensive trade with other countries. Ambassadors, messengers and jewelers traveled by sea. They ended up in such faraway ports as China.

The ancient Egyptians also referred to Cush as "Ta-Seti" or "the land of the bow."[10] The nation produced skilled archers who were conscripted as mercenaries in the armed forces of many different nations. The ancient Israeli army had Cushite soldiers within its ranks. It was a black soldier named Cushi who was sent to King David to relate the awful news of his son Absalom's demise (2 Sam 18:19-21).

Four hundred years later, in the exodus from Egypt, Moses led a crowd that consisted of more than 400,000 people. Where did they come from? The Bible calls them a "mixed multitude" (Ex 12:37-38). Many of those who fled the bitterness of Egyptian slavery with Moses might have been Cushites. Moses himself married a black woman (Num 12:1). Aaron, his brother, had a son named Phineas, which is translated "the Negro," or "the black."[11] Later, Eli, the high priest of Israel and Samuel's mentor, had a son by the same name.[12]

There was another African woman of some renown mentioned in the Old Testament. She came from a faraway land to commune with the wisest man on the face of the earth. She was impressed by his industrious ways. He was a monarch engaged in an ambitious building campaign. She was a world power in her own right. The Jewish historian Josephus called her "the Queen of Egypt and Ethiopia."[13] The Bible calls her "the Queen of Sheba."

The Israeli King Rehoboam refused to walk in the ways of his God. In his fifth year in office he had a fearsome visitor in the person of King Shishak of Egypt. Shishak's calling card was a regiment of twelve hundred chariots and sixty thousand horsemen. Many

Cushite soldiers marched within the ranks of Shishak's army when he entered Jerusalem. The Bible says that he took everything, including the gold shield Solomon had made.[14]

The Bible speaks of a mighty African general named Zerah the Cushite (2 Chron 14:9-15). Sometime between 913 and 873 B.C., he marched against the kingdom of Judah. Israel's King Asa was terrified as advance surveillance reports came in. Zerah had an army of perhaps a million men. Three hundred charioteers bolstered his armed soldiers. Historians believe that Zerah might have been a Cushite general in the services of Pharaoh Orsorkon I (924-889 B.C.).[15]

As early as the twelfth century B.C., Egyptian records of military campaigns against the Cushite people began to appear. Egypt's thirteenth dynasty left a cartouche of a king named Ra-Neshi or "the Negro of Ra." (Amon-Ra was an Egyptian deity.) Ra-Neshi ruled in the Egyptian delta region.[16]

At the close of Egypt's eighteenth dynasty, Pharaoh Ahmose complained of a political crisis which threatened his rule. He wrote: "Let me understand what this strength is for! [One] prince is in Avaris, another is in Ethiopia [Cush] and [here] I sit associated with an Asiatic and a Negro [Neshi]! Each man has his slice of this Egypt, dividing up the land with me. I can not pass by him as far as Memphis."[17]

Secrets of El Kurru

Today in the barren wasteland which was once Cush, there lies a cemetery that has defied time. It lies undisturbed beneath the crumbling ruins of a Cushite pyramid. Thirty-six royal tombs occupy this place. They contain the embalmed remains of the nation's royalty. In another day, in another time, these men and women of renown rode proudly on horseback through the streets of Thebes and Meroe, bowing slightly to acknowledge the cheering masses.

King Piankhi was a religious man. He was a faithful adherent to the tenets of the Egyptian deity Amon-Ra. Piankhi was also the sovereign ruler of the land of Cush. At the close of Egypt's twenty-fourth dynasty, he led his forces north. They overran the city of Memphis. Many of the Egyptians surrendered peacefully in the face of Piankhi's superior military machine. Pharaoh Orsorkon IV surrendered at Heliopolis.[18] When the Cushites took that city, the local ruler's wife led a delegation to Piankhi's camp. They threw themselves down and begged Piankhi to spare the city.[19]

Piankhi savored the moment of victory. At the height of conquest he strode majestically into the temple of Amon. As the frightened priests huddled in the shadows, the new pharaoh of Egypt walked into the sacred place, the very Holy of Holies. The priests fell down on their faces in obeisance. Piankhi had a huge monument erected to celebrate his conquest. The inscription read, "Amon of Thebes has made me sovereign over Egypt."[20] (In actuality, a large portion of Egypt remained unconquered.)

Shabaka was Piankhi's younger brother. He was also his successor to the throne. Under his rule the Cushites succeeded in conquering the remaining portion of Egypt. Shabaka sat on the royal throne at Thebes, as would his son Shabataka. Shabataka established diplomatic alliances with both Israel and Syria. Those treaties would lead to hostile relations with the ruthless Assyrian army.

The King of Israel Pleads for Cushite Help

King Hezekiah was in trouble. The most powerful army on earth had attacked Judah. Sennacherib of Assyria had made the Israelites victims of his royal extortion racket. He demanded huge sums from Israel and its king. The Palestinian monarch sent back a hastily worded letter to Sennacherib. It said, "I have done no wrong. Withdraw from me and I will pay whatever you demand of me" (2 Kings 18:14).

In desperation King Hezekiah raided the temple treasury. He even stripped the gold from the temple doorposts. He had these riches loaded up and sent to Sennacherib (2 Kings 18:15-16). How long would this treasure appease the appetites of a tyrant who had conquered so much of the known world? After an inspiring moment of prayer, Hezekiah sent a messenger bursting through the gates of Jerusalem on horseback. His envoy was carrying a desperate plea for help.

Sennacherib sneered. He warned the Israelites, "Do not let Hezekiah persuade you to trust in the LORD when he says, 'The LORD will deliver us; the city will not be given into the hand of the king of Assyria'" (2 Kings 18:30).

Pharaoh Shabaka moved decisively once King Hezekiah's plea was received. He summoned his twenty-year-old nephew Tarharka to the throne. Tarharka was the general of the entire Cushite/Egyptian military regime. Statues and figurines show us Tarharka's classical

Negroid features. He had a broad nose, thick lips and full cheeks. His face had a rich chocolate complexion. Once apprised of the urgency of the matter, he took off toward Palestine. The thunder of thousands of marching feet followed in his wake.

A shout of joy went up when Tarharka's legions marched into view. Young boys and girls hollered and waved at the battalions of black-skinned, battle-ready soldiers. Some of the warriors already bore the scars of battle. Others were ready to be tested on the field of combat.

The Bible tells us that the "angel of the LORD" visited the Assyrian camp that night and killed eighty-five thousand Assyrian troops (2 Kings 19:35). Some scholars believe that a plague decimated the Assyrian ranks. Whatever the case, Sennacherib woke up the next morning to the stunning news that he would have to run for his life. A fragment from a clay table found by archaeologists suggests that Pharaoh Shabaka and King Sennacherib might have signed a peace treaty before the latter was murdered by his own sons.[21]

The Fall of the Twenty-Fifth Dynasty

Tarharka sent for his mother in 689 B.C. She traveled twelve hundred miles from Cush to Memphis to attend his coronation—the general was to be crowned as the new pharaoh.[22] Tarharka was a patron of the arts. He also invested heavily in the rebuilding of the Egyptian holy places.

Around 671 B.C. Egypt was attacked by the Assyrian army.[23] The Assyrians had possession of iron weapons, which the Cushites had yet to develop. The Cushites lost all of Egypt except Upper Egypt and the city of Thebes. Eshahaddon, Sennacherib's son, sacked and pillaged the city of Memphis. Tarharka's successor lost the rest of Egypt. The carnage was awful. The Assyrian ruler recalled: "Against Egypt and [Cush] I have let my weapons rage and showed my might."[24]

The prophet Nahum used the destruction of Cush as a warning to the Ninevites. He said, "Are you better than Thebes, situated on the Nile, with water around her? The river was her defense, the waters her wall. Cush and Egypt were her boundless strength; Put and Libya were among her allies. Yet she was taken captive and went into exile. Her infants were dashed to pieces at the head of every street. Lots were cast for her nobles, and all her great men were put in chains" (Nahum 3:8-10).

In 1928 historian Sir Arthur Weigally referred to Egypt's twenty-fifth dynasty as the "epoch of nigger domination."[25] In 1970 Egyptologist J. E. White Manchip called the Cushites "simple blacks."[26] The scholar later remarked, "Perhaps as Negroes they felt ill at ease among the fair-skinned Egyptians."[27] He claimed that after leaving Egypt "they quickly reverted to a savage mode of life."[28] Hardly. While the Cushites never again conquered Egypt, they continued to live at a high standard of civilization. Meroe became Cush's capital sometime after 6 B.C. The city was centrally located near key trading routes.[29] It boasted of a thriving iron works center. Both Greeks and Romans traveled to Cush to see its splendor.

Black mercenaries from Cush continued to serve in the Egyptian armies. They waged war against Greece and Rome. Black soldiers entered Cyprus during an Egyptian military expedition sometime between 568 and 525 B.C. Huge stone statues of black men found in that region attest to their ancient presence there.[30]

A Cushite contingent warred for the Persian army under King Xerxes. Their awesome presence in leopard- and lion-skin clothings was recorded for posterity. It was said that they used stone-tipped arrows.[31]

Hannibal, the mighty conqueror of Carthage, turned to the blacks of Cush for help during his famed campaign. It must have been quite a sight as black men mounted the backs of elephants and braved the snow-capped Alps to conquer Italy. The Carthaginians had a coin struck to commemorate the event. It was imprinted with an elephant on one side and the face of a black man on the other.[32]

Ebed-Melek was a high official in King Zedekiah of Israel's palace. Jeremiah was a prophet of God in trouble. His stark, angry prophecies about Israel's impending judgment found no welcome in the king's court. Jeremiah was sentenced and thrown into a huge pit. Ebed-Melek was moved to action upon hearing of his plight. He enlisted a contingent of the royal guard and pulled the prophet out of the pit. In return, Jeremiah promised that his life would be spared after Israel fell. Ebed-Melek was a black Hebrew.[33]

Was Jesus Black?
There is a man hanging in the shadows of Golgotha, the place of the skull. Thick, ominous clouds frame the backdrop of his death scene.

The instrument of his public execution is a large, wooden T-shaped object. He writhes in agony, struggling to raise himself up for one more precious gulp of air.

A woman watches from the closest distance that the Roman soldiers will allow. She wears a veil drawn tightly over her face. Yet the physical resemblance between her and the man on the cross is remarkable. She falls to her knees, a ball of anguish and pain. She is his mother. Her name is Mary.

What is his name? "His name shall be called Jesus," an angel once proclaimed, "for he shall save his people from their sins" (Mt 1:21).

To be sure, the significance of this precious life far transcends the boundaries of ethnicity. The gift of his shed blood frees from the condemnation of sin any person who receives him. God did live among us as a human. To say that Jesus was raceless, colorless and devoid of a native culture only cheapens the gospel narrative.

Jesus never exalted his culture or ethnicity above his relationship with the Father. However, he never denied his heritage as a son of David. Through the inspiration of the Holy Spirit, the record of his genealogy was transcribed for posterity. Let us look at the African roots of the Savior.

In *Black Biblical Presence,* Walter McCray writes concerning the ethnicity of several women listed in Jesus' genealogy. He mentions Tamar the daughter-in-law of Judah, a Canaanite woman, as one of his ancestors. Rahab, the prostitute who aided the two Hebrew spies, Caleb and Joshua, gave birth to a son named Boaz. Both she and her son were related to Jesus. McCray's book also lists Bathsheba, Solomon's mother, as a possible African ancestor of Jesus.[34]

In *What Color Was Jesus?* William Moseley writes, "If there was assimilation of black peoples among the Israelites, and there was; and if Jesus was an Israelite, and He was; then Jesus might have very well inherited genes from Ethiopian ancestors, which would have made him black."[35]

Jesus' ancestry would not have designated him a full-blooded African. However, most African-American people have some mixture of heritage within their genealogies. For the largest part of the African-American's sojourn in the United States, the slightest trace of the African blood has classified one as a black person. Today, African-Americans whose complexions are so light that they are sometimes mistaken for Caucasians are considered black in America. When slavery reigned in American life, even a single distant black ancestor condemned one to a life of slavery. When Jim Crow laws segregated African-Americans, a single drop of black blood relegated a United States citizen to the back of the bus.

If Jesus had lived in America when slavery was practiced, his African blood would have condemned him to cotton field slavery. If he had lived during the height of legalized segregation, his skin color might have denied him access to many Christian churches. If Jesus Christ walked the earth today in human form, he might yet be segregated into the killing fields of a North American ghetto.

The Integrated Church
The early church was a racially integrated institution. Many different groups were represented on the day of Pentecost when the Holy Spirit descended upon the saints in the upper room (Acts 2:5-11). The church at Antioch had a least two African members in leadership: Simeon, who was also called Niger, and Lucius of Cyrene (Acts 13:1).

The first Gentile convert to Christianity was black. The Holy Spirit led the evangelist Philip into the wilderness where he came across a foreign dignitary riding in the passenger seat of a chauffeur-driven chariot (Acts 8:26-40). The "Ethiopian eunuch," as history has labeled him, was reading from the book of Isaiah. Philip approached the man and helped him to draw the correlation between the words of Isaiah and the recently resurrected Messiah, Jesus Christ. The Cushite finance minister probably rode back to the capital city of Meroe rejoicing that he had found God in the desert.

What is certain is that some of the great thinkers and apologists of the Christian faith were Africans: Names like Tertullian, Cyprian, Augustine and Athanasius shaped Christian thought and reason for the ages to come.

2

●●

Black West Africa

Once there was a world of courageous knights and evil warlords, a world of immense and indescribable wealth, of greed, of emperors and dynasties, a world where the blazing sun gleamed from the tip of the double-edged saber, a land of mercenaries, of pirates, of royal palaces ornate with golden fixtures and velvet carpeting, a world with tens of thousands of cavalry soldiers armed with shield, bow and arrow.

Once there was a world where the legions of warriors would gladly give their lives in the service of the king, a world where on a cool summer night, royal knights serenaded black-skinned, kinky-haired princesses. This was a world of high culture, of major universities, plush gardens and tree-lined gardens. In antiquity this was the world of West Africa.

Historian John Henrik Clarke states: "Before the breaking up of the social structure of the West African states of Ghana, Mali, Songhai and the internal strife and chaos that made the slave trade possible, the forefathers of the Africans who eventually became the slaves in the United States lived in a society where university life was fairly common and scholars were beheld with reverence."[1]

The Empire of Ghana
The war-horses snorted as the acrid, bitter scent of burning filled their flaring nostrils. The sounds of shouting and revelry filled the streets

of Ghana's major cities. The Muslim invaders from the north had overrun Ghana's borders. The Almoravids, desert people from the northern regions, pronounced *jihad* (holy war) on the ailing empire called Ghana. By 1076, Ghana's capital city was in Almoravid hands. Tears ran down the dark brown faces of the empire's great leaders. Ghana the mighty had fallen.[2]

Ancient Ghana had been the first of the great civilizations of Western Africa. It extended from the Niger River to the Atlantic seaboard, then reached upward into the Sahara desert. The outposts of the empire merged into a state around A.D. 300. It reached its political height in the eleventh century—shortly before its collapse.[3]

Ghana is remembered largely for its immense wealth. Toward the end of the eighth century, al-Fazari and other Arab geographers began to call it "the land of gold." One writer said this of its king: "[He] is the wealthiest of kings on the face of the earth on account of the riches he owns and the hoards of gold acquired by him and inherited by him and inherited from his predecessors since ancient time."

The name *Ghana* meant "war chief." It was the honorary title bestowed upon the kings of the nation. However, the outside world began to refer to the country itself as Ghana.

King Fettasi was the king of the Ghana at the end of the seventh century. He owned a royal stable which housed a thousand horses. A silk rope led each of them. There were three attendants for each of his horses.[4]

Ghana's main enterprise was trade. The country was centrally located at a crossroads point that caravans had to cross to find both salt and gold. The people to the south had the gold supply, but they lacked salt. The people to the north produced salt to trade for gold. Ghana played the part of the middle man, charging import and export taxes on both gold and salt.

Traders from North Africa came to Ghana's famous markets to buy gold, slaves, ivory, kola nuts, honey, gums and cotton. They traded salt, copper, dried fruit and cloth. The merchants from the north also brought their religion with them. They introduced Islam to West Africa. By 1067, Islam had become a major force in Ghana.

Ghana had a strong administrative government that ensured the safety of the traders and merchants within its borders. The capital city of the king was called Kumbi Saleh. It was the largest West African city of its day. In fact, writer Ibn Khaldoun described it as one of the most highly populated cities in the world.[5] Kumbi Saleh was divided into two separate townships which were six miles apart. They were separated by a valley. One of the cities was a Muslim settlement. The other city was known for its worship of the local deities.

One of the townships was named el-Ghaba ("the forest"). The king of Ghana made his residence here. It is said that the king's palace, made of stone, was adorned with works of art and windows of glass.

Kumbi Saleh's other province was a settlement for Muslim business people. It had twelve mosques and many theologians who gave spiritual guidance to Islam's adherents. Each mosque had imams, muezzins and salaried reciters of the Koran.

The king was a powerful figure in the Ghanaian political structure. His subjects would gather at his palaces when the sound of drums echoed through the kingdom. Guard dogs with gold and silver collars stood watch at his gates. Al-Bakri wrote:

> When the king gives audience to his people, to listen to their complaints and to set them to rights, he sits in a pavilion around which stand ten pages holding shields and gold-mounted swords. On his right hand are the sons of the princes of his empire, splendidly clad and with gold plaiting in their hair. The governor of the city is seated on the ground in front of the king, and all around him are his counselors in the same position.[6]

The wealth of the country became known throughout the world. At its peak, Ghana's borders surrounded 250,000 miles of real estate. As the legend of the empire spread, Ghana needed a strong standing army to protect its extensive resources. By the eleventh century, Ghana's king could put 200,000 troops into the field on short notice. By 1060 he also had 40,000 archers poised for battle. In comparison, the Norman army which conquered England in A.D. 1066 had only 15,000 men.[7]

However, the end was coming. When the Almoravids sacked Kumbi Saleh, the writer Ibn Kahldoun came down to weigh a prized Ghanaian gold nugget. It was said to have weighed close to a ton.[8]

The Rise of the Empire of Mali
By 1230 the Almoravid threat had passed and Ghana had regained a measure of self-government. But trouble was brewing. One of the

country's vassal states revolted. The Sosso people waged war against Ghana.

Sumanguru was the ruler of the Sosso people. He thought that it was dangerous to keep the sons of the previous rulers around. He killed eleven of them but spared one, a frail, crippled child named Sundiata. Perhaps Sumanguru reasoned that the youth would never be able to pose a threat to him. He was mistaken. Sundiata somehow gained the use of his legs and learned to walk. He eventually stood tall enough to wrest the throne from Sosso. The kingdom of Mali was established under his rule.

A series of rulers ascended to the throne after Sundiata's death. One of them was Sakura, a man who had been a slave in the royal house. One day he saw his chance—and seized the throne. But Sakura was eventually assassinated in Somaliland.[9]

Mansa Musa ascended to the throne of Mali's empire in 1312. He conquered the Berber cities of the western desert. He also extended the borders of Mali northward into what are present-day Mauritania and southern Algeria. Mali extended to the Hausa states of Nigeria in the south.[10]

A substantial cotton crop was harvested in Mali. Many people in the kingdom were employed as blacksmiths, goldsmiths, silversmiths and coppersmiths. Tanners and dyers also made a living in Mansa Musa's Mali.

Islam's influence had been strongly felt in West Africa for many years. However it was Mansa Musa who made Islam the state religion. He himself was a very pious Muslim. During his reign he promoted the founding of Koranic schools as well as the compulsory study of the Koran. He sent students of promise to Morocco and Egypt to further their studies. Mansa Musa built mosques all over his kingdom.

Sheikh Abu Sa'id Otman ed Dukkali described Musa as the sultan of the land of "the desert of gold." He said,

> The sultan of this kingdom presides in his palace on a great balcony called *bembe,* where he has a great seat of ebony that is a throne fit for a large and tall person: on either side it is flanked by elephant tusks turned toward each other. His arms stand near him, being all gold, saber, lance, quiver, bow and arrows. He wears trousers made of twenty pieces [of cloth], of a kind which he alone can wear.[11]

Mansa Musa's Great Hajj

Adherents to the Islamic faith are encouraged by religious duty to make *hajj* (pilgrimage) to the ancient city of Mecca in Egypt. Bound by his belief in Allah, Mansa Musa prepared himself to make the trip to Egypt. His visit left so deep an impression in Egypt that Egyptian chroniclers recorded it as one of the principal events of A.D. 1324.[12]

On the morning when travel was to begin, Mansa Musa mounted his white Arabian horse. He must have smiled to himself as he looked at the procession that followed him. Five hundred slaves followed on foot, each of them carrying a gold staff that weighed five or six pounds. Eighty camels walked with his entourage. Each of them carried three hundred pounds of gold dust. Other camels carried food and other provisions.[13]

The emperor also took with him soldiers, luggage handlers, royal secretaries, doctors, teachers and local politicians. There were 10,000 horses and riders. In all, he was followed by about 100,000 subjects.

Musa was received in Cairo as the great sultan. Though he spoke perfect Arabic, he would speak only through an interpreter. Al-Makrizi recalled that Musa was a young man with "brown skin." He said that Musa "had a pleasant face with a good figure. . . . He appeared amidst his companions magnificently dressed. . . . He brought gifts and presents that amazed the eye with their beauty and splendor."[14]

Ol-Mari wrote of Mansa Musa:

> He is the most important of the Muslim Negro kings, his land is the largest, his army the most numerous, he is the king who is most powerful, the richest, the most fortunate, the most feared by his enemies, the most able to good to those around him.[15]

The emperor gave gold to his new friends. He gave it to government officials. He gave it to poor people whom he met along his way. Mansa Musa gave away so much gold during his *hajj* that the market crashed. It took twelve years for Egypt's economy to recover.[16]

It is said that Mansa Musa purchased properties in Mecca and Cairo so that lodging could be provided for future pilgrimages. The emperor exchanged ambassadors with several foreign nations. He returned to Mali with architects from North Africa who would work in his kingdom. The kingdom of Mali eventually grew to ten million people.

Musa's *hajj* put Mali on the map, literally. King Charles V of France had Musa's picture drawn on a 1339 world map.[17] The etching depicted Musa as a bearded black man with royal robes, a crown and a scepter, holding a gigantic gold nugget in one of his hands. A hundred years later, Europeans would use that map as they came searching for Musa's gold.

The Songhai Empire

Mansa Musa died in 1337. By the fifteenth century, Mali was collapsing. Invaders from other lands eventually captured huge chunks of its property. As Mali's power disintegrated, a small state known as Gao declared its independence. A fledgling monarch named Sunni Ali was fundamentally responsible for transforming Gao into the empire of Songhai. Sunni Ali came to the throne in 1464. A large royal court surrounded him. He sat on a raised platform which was encircled by seven hundred eunuchs. A master of wardrobe took charge of his attire. An imperial council dealt with the empire's affair. A chancellor secretary took minutes and dispersed the emperor's correspondence.[18]

Sunni Ali the Great raised up a strong military regiment that would insure that Gao was not recolonized by Mali. He drafted soldiers from vassal states. He also created a navy of two thousand war canoes that sailed up and down the Nile River.

The crown owned the largest slave settlements in the empire. It filled the ranks of its standing army with its pool of forced laborers. The unfortunates served as bow men for the Songhai army. The Songhai cavalry was composed of free men. They had lances and sabres with which to defend themselves. Horses outfitted with iron breastplates were imported from the Berber states and Portugal.[19]

In 1468 Songhai annexed the trading city of Timbuktu. It was Mansa Musa who had originally established Timbuktu as a great center of learning. On his pilgrimage to Mecca he enlisted some of the great scholars of the Islamic world to return to West Africa as instructors. However, the city of Timbuktu flourished during the Songhai dynasty. Timbuktu was so rich from trade that it was known as "the golden city." Located at the northern end of the Niger River, Timbuktu was a city with tree-lined streets and boulevards. It was a haven for tradespeople, merchants and scholars—an intellectual center that was famous for its libraries. Scholars came to Timbuktu from far and near to study at the University of Sankore. They studied astronomy, mathematics, ethnography, medicine and hygiene. Courses were also offered in philosophy, theology, exegesis, diction, elocution and rhetoric.[20]

* * *

In 1492, a Spanish explorer named Christopher Columbus landed in the Americas. Europeans were already actively trading on the West African coastlands. A page of West African history was turning.

Part Two

· ·

From African Kingdoms to American Slavery

*H*arlem, New York, is called the capital of black America. The sprawling colony in upper Manhattan is a microcosm of the African diaspora. Its sidewalks are filled with Southern-born blacks, West Indian blacks, Canadian blacks, African-born blacks and native Harlem-born blacks. Harlemites are a kaleidoscope of skin tones: they range in complexion from light caramel to the deepest brown. Most of these people are descendants of black people who once crossed the Atlantic Ocean in the holds of slave ships.

The African holocaust was one of the bloodiest tragedies ever visited upon humanity. The slave trade could be described as the tears of orphaned children in African villages, their parents kidnapped and gone forever. The slave trade was the forgotten dead pitched from slave ships, thrown to the sharks. The slave trade was corroded smiles and back room deals. It was papal blessings—and pain and bloodshed for the enslaved.

Slavery was not a new institutional system when the people of Europe arrived in West Africa. However, they gave it a new twist. The captives who were brought to the New World were stripped of their cultures, native tongues and history. All self-identity was destroyed as the master sought to control the slave's mind as well as body.

The economy of a new nation called the United States was built on the sweaty, aching, whip-scarred backs of the African slaves. Their free labor helped build the infrastructure of the country and transform it rapidly into a world power.

Slavery has been referred to as America's "original sin." Its legacy of segregation and racial mistrust shackles black-white relations today. In Part Two we will examine slavery and black humanity's life in the New World—a story of weeping, work and war.

3

. . . .

Slavemakers

*A*nd it was night. The cool breezes of evening swept across a fishing community on the coast of West Africa in A.D. 1441. The white, sandy beaches were empty in the moonlight, devoid of anything but the footprints of the children who had played there earlier that day.

An eerie silence played around the homes that made up the village. All was still. Then, suddenly, there was a stir. A woman's scream shattered the night like a hammer striking plate glass. The humid air filled with sounds of running feet and heavy gasps for breath. Unknown men were yelling in a strange tongue.

And then there was fire. Mothers and fathers snatched their children from their beds and began to flee. Men with white skin ran back and forth carrying torches. Orange flames danced with the stars in the night sky. Thatch-roofed homes quickly fell prey to the fire.

This was the European's first verified interaction with the native West Africans. That night a band of Portuguese soldiers under the command of Antonio Golsalves and Nuno Tristan raided two villages. The fire had been a diversionary tactic. Twelve of the West African villagers were kidnapped and taken back to Portugal by force. Others were killed during the attack.

Prince Henry the Navigator, Portugal's ruler, was delighted to receive his loyal subjects from their royal journey. He was even more joyous to receive the black slaves and the small amount of gold dust that the sailors had been able to procure in West Africa. These imports meant that his mission had met with success. Pope Martin V also rejoiced. Some of the slaves were sent to serve at his residence. Armed with church-awarded sovereignty over all lands east of Cape Blanco, West Africa, Prince Henry was ready to send out another expedition.[1]

Prior to the landing on the West African coast, Portugal was on the freeway to economic ruin. As a Christian nation it lacked access to the Muslim-dominated trading centers of North Africa. The destiny of Portugal lay in its ability to challenge the Muslim blockade and establish trade in the region. Early on, the Portuguese discovered that the Muslims did not control the gold-producing regions of West Africa. They hoped to find the source of the gold and establish direct trade with the countries that controlled the enterprise.

Tales of a powerful gold-rich Christian ruler from West Africa also reached the ears of Prince Henry the Navigator. Legend had it that Prester John was a benevolent man who ruled a huge kingdom with a great military force. The Portuguese hoped to locate the monarch and enlist his aid in a war against the North African Muslims. Prince Henry's sailors never found Prester John, but they did find the gold. And they found another valuable commodity: black human beings.

True, the Portuguese originally came to Africa in search of gold. However, a substantial number of Africans were soon being sent to Portugal yearly to be sold. Slave traders began to arrive from other European nations. Slaves were stolen by people like the Brandenburgers and the Dutch, English and French. The opening of the New World territories created a further appetite for slave laborers. Black sinews were needed to conquer the dense foliage of a faraway wilderness called "America."

The Europeans Find Partners

The Europeans began their slave-making expeditions by kidnapping Africans themselves, but these kidnapping forays rarely yielded more than a few human beings. The sailors needed hundreds to fill a ship. But when they attempted to enter the interior of Africa, Europeans fell victim to diseases like malaria, and their expeditions were sometimes met by poison arrows. Inner Africa came to be known as "the white man's grave." Early on, Europeans began diplomatic relationships with the kings who controlled the nation states of West Africa.

African monarchs like the Damel of Cayor controlled large sections of the African coastlands. The Damel had a two-thousand-man infantry. Two hundred knights in armor also protected his interests. The Damel was treacherous in his dealings, often selling his own subjects into slavery. He became proficient at playing one European nation against another.[2]

The Damel of Cayor was just one African ruler who found that slavery could be a profitable enterprise on both sides of the Atlantic Ocean. Richard Olaniyan writes, "The Europeans did not go into the interior to capture slaves but maintained forts and trading stations along the coast of West Africa where kings and chiefs came to sell or barter their own slaves and certain categories of criminals and war captives." One European trader reported in 1680, "The great wealth of the Fantineans [Fanti] makes them so proud and haughty that any European trading there must stand bare to them." Some African kings were escorted to Europe and treated lavishly by European monarchs.[3]

Slavery Becomes Big Business

The future of West Africa was being written in blood. Canoes loaded down with scared, whimpering men and women slithered through the humid air of the interior. They floated through mosquito-infested waterways and conduits, headed for the trading centers at the coast. Warriors with pistols, rifles and mounted cannon kept a keen eye out for interlopers.

Black captives also marched across the red clay of well-traveled African trade routes. Coffles—groups of slaves tied or chained together in a line—walked sometimes five hundred miles to their destination.[4] The way was littered with human skulls and unanswered prayers. The march took months and sometimes years.

Slave Castles

On January 20, 1482, the Portuguese began construction of the first slave "factory" in West Africa. It was established on the what had become known as the Gold Coast. The Portuguese called the castle El Mina or "the mine." There was no mine at El Mina. The mines were located inland, and access to their general location was denied to the

Europeans. The place was named El Mina because the region itself was rich in gold. A local monarch leased the parcel of property where the factory was built to the Portuguese government.[5]

That slave castle still stands on the beachhead of West Africa. Cannons were placed on the roof parapets to protect against ambitious slavers from other nations. Dark, foul-smelling dungeons were constructed below. The men were assigned to one stone-floored holding pen, women and children to another. A special windowless compartment was constructed for rebellious slaves. Slave ships drifted just a few feet from its infamous "door of no return." Once the indigenous people walked through the door of the "slave factory," they were not seen again.

See the loading process through the eyes of an African queen:

> Suddenly a group of priests appeared . . . [as] uncomprehending captives were herded past them, the fathers swung containers of holy water. "Your name is Peter; your name is John; yours is Francis." The priests on the dock made a last gesture of blessing and guards began to push the slaves below deck.[6]

The queen watched as some captives jumped overboard. The heavy chains caused them to sink to the bottom of the ocean. Other captives were clubbed into submission and herded down below deck.

Traders used two different types of cargo methods in storing their human freight. They called the ships "loose packers" and "tight packers." Loose packers allowed the slave breathing room and freedom of movement. Tight packers used every available space to store a brown body. Slaves barely had room to turn around. Poor ventilation and noxious fumes made breathing difficult.

One slave described the accommodations below the deck. "The wretched situation was again aggravated by the galling of the chain, now became insupportable; and the filth of the necessary tubs [commodes] into which the children fell, and were almost suffocated. The shrieks of the women and dying rendered the whole scene of horror almost inconceivably."[7]

In 1781 the crew of the British slave vessel, the Zong, found themselves short of supplies. Delays had put a strain on the food and water staples. All on board could not be fed. Insurance companies would reimburse slave-ship investors for slaves who died in transit. So the crewmen grabbed 132 African captives and pitched them over the side of the ship. The healthiest slaves were spared for future sale.[8]

Africans in the Americas

Sir John Hawkins had the dubious distinction of becoming the first slave-ship captain to bring Africans to the Americas. Hawkins was a religious gentleman who insisted that his crew "serve God daily" and "love another." His ship, ironically called "the good ship Jesus," left the shores of his native England for Africa in October 1562. He arrived at Sierra Leone, and in a short time he had three hundred blacks in his possession. Hawkins claimed to have acquired them "partly by sword and partly by other means."[9]

Hawkins took part in "the Great Circuit," also known as "the triangle trade." He purchased cheap products from England with which to barter for slaves in Africa. He obtained slaves in Africa and exchanged them in the West Indies for raw materials and foodstuffs to take back to England. From time to time African monarchs would enlist Europeans as allies against foreign powers. Hawkins was approached for such help. Hawkins's "help" came neither free nor cheap. He was a mercenary. He once served the king of Sierra Leone and the king of the Castros in a large-scale military operative. Two hundred Englishmen fought alongside the African troops. For his role in the conquest, John Hawkins was awarded the proceeds from the sale of all of the 470 prisoners of war.[10]

Queen Elizabeth frowned on Hawkins's activity. She said, "It was detestable and would call down vengeance from heaven upon the undertakers." However, the flesh was weak. One look at Sir John Hawkins's ledger books turned the queen into an investor.[11]

Fighting the Power

Some West African kingdoms resisted the slave trade. Queen Nzinga of Angola confronted the Portuguese who had ravaged her country by slave-hunting. Nzinga created an alliance with the Jaga kings. As a unified force they shut down the Portuguese trade routes and confined the whites to the slave castles on the coast. The queen finally fled with her rebel forces to Matamaba. Her guerilla warfare tactics caused many a restless night for the Portuguese. Nzinga was twice baptized as a Christian. When she died in 1663, she was buried with a crucifix around her neck and a bow and arrow in her hand.[12]

The slave trade became a major economic industry in West Africa. The magnitude of it expanded to overwhelming proportions. Entire nations were depopulated. Thousands were exported to foreign lands. The proud black people of the Asante, Dahomey, Oyo, Fanti, Mossi and Mandinka kingdoms were just some of those who ended up in the bottom of slave ships.

The nation-states of West Africa became increasingly militarized. By 1500 the kingdom of Benin was hiring Portuguese mercenaries to bolster its armed forces. By the 1700s Birmingham, England, gunsmiths were pouring 100,000 to 150,000 guns a year into West Africa.[13]

The Europeans traded guns for slaves. Guns soon became a necessity to a sovereign nation. If a nation did not have guns, it could be enslaved by its neighbors. Basil Davidson writes:

> [The Asante] were seldom or never willing to sell their own people: hence they had to conquer foreign states, since other African nations, in the same game, controlled the trade routes to the coast. This in turn needed more firearms; and more firearms called for more slaves. Thus, Asante grew into one of the strongest slaving nations of Africa.... Questions of power and wealth apart, slavery had become the price of Asante survival.[14]

Aftermath of the Holocaust

Slavery began to inflict tremendous adverse affects on the African continent. Some estimate that Africa lost between fifty and a hundred million Africans to the European-American slave trade. Maulana Karenga said, "The holocaust caused the loss of youth and skilled personnel, thus affecting the scientific, technological and cultural progress of Africa."[15]

The West Africans thought largely in terms of kindred, clan and tribe. They spoke different languages. They did not see themselves as members of a larger group that encompassed all black people. They and their descendants first began to understand their interrelatedness as a result of the common lot they shared: the horror of the slave trade.

Africans began to appear in a wide range of diverse places. Peru, Brazil, Cuba, Barbados, Jamaica, Haiti, Puerto Rico and other Western-hemisphere countries used slave labor to build their economies. The Dutch, the English, the Spanish and the French imported huge slave armies to work their sugar and tobacco plantations.

Culture shock for the forced refugees was dramatic. Men and women were kidnapped and bartered for in West Africa. They arrived in chains in another part of the world three months later. Some blacks went mad. The change in climate killed off some slaves. Despondent blacks committed suicide. Some captives ran off from their plantations and died of exposure. Those who survived these maladies were soon to learn the ways of the New World.

The slave masters of the West Indies found themselves enmeshed in a serious dilemma. By 1673 there were only eight thousand whites in Jamaica. The number of slaves had risen to ten thousand.[16] This phenomenon happened in many of the European settlements. What would stop the slaves from uprising and exacting revenge on their oppressors?

A process called "seasoning" was implemented. By means of torture, freeborn human beings were transformed into chattel. The slave codes facilitated this process. The first time a bondsperson struck a "Christian," he was whipped. The second offense was branding on the face with a hot iron. In Antigua in 1687, a rebellious slave had his tongue pulled out and his leg cut off as "a living example to the rest."[17]

Flogging was reserved for insolent or defiant slaves. The whip could inflict a hole in the flesh large enough that a person's finger could be inserted into it. A common punishment was to hoist the offender from a tree with weights tied to the neck and waist.

Seasoning was designed to spoil the offender's resolve. Sixteen- to eighteen-hour workdays would cause the slaves to wear out. Seasoning also killed them. Thirty percent of the slaves brought to the West Indies died. The aristocracy didn't mind. The profits were so high that more could be imported. Soon more money would be realized as a new market was about to open—a market called America.

4

Slavery in the United States of America

*I*n the shadow of President George Washington's noble Mount Vernon estate sat rows of ramshackle wooden shacks. Beyond, black men and women, the children of West Africa, labored in his fields as the blazing noonday sun beat down. The smell of manure burned in their nostrils as they scattered it among the crops. A fourteen-year-old girl guided a donkey with a plow.[1]

George Washington's regard for the more than three hundred slaves who called him "master" was debatable. He was not above ordering a good beating for a disobedient slave.[2] However, he usually did not waste his time. He knew what frightened his captives into submission: The slaves feared a one way trip to West Indies as much as many people fear hell. The climate, the numerous diseases and the severe treatment killed slaves even faster than the rigors of President Washington's plantation. The threat became a reality for one of Washington's slaves named Tom. The father of American liberty traded him to the West Indies for some dinner table dainties.[3]

Thomas Jefferson and the Slavery Issue

Thomas Jefferson was another architect of American freedom. He composed the phrase "all men are created equal." His Monticello, Virginia, estate was the talk of the high society set. His gang of slaves built it from the ground up.[4]

Jefferson's slaves found him often generous with gifts of food, clothes and even money. He was also an austere man. The whip was wielded frequently and brutally on his estate. Some slaves ran away to escape the torment.

When money problems arose, Thomas Jefferson sold off his most defiant slaves to balance his books. He remembered them only as names and birth dates in a ledger. In 1796, thanks to natural reproduction, Jefferson still had 167 black people in captivity.[5]

Slavery in the Land of the Free

Patrick Henry will forever be remembered as one of the fathers of the American revolution. One of his biographers called him a "flaming apostle of American democracy."

On May 20, 1775, Henry made a speech which is part of the American canon. He passionately expressed his dissatisfaction with Britain's rule over the American colonies. He said, "Is life so dear, or peace so sweet, as to be purchased at the price of chains and slavery? Forbid it, Almighty God. I know not what course others may take; but as for me, give me liberty or give me death!"

He left his moment of glory to return to his plantation home. On the front porch of the "big house," house slaves fanned his brow and brought him cool mint juleps as he read the evening newspaper. For all of his talk of liberty, Henry was one of the largest slaveholders in the country. Eventually someone asked him how he could justify fighting for American freedom while denying freedom to his slaves. Patrick Henry answered, "I am drawn along by the general inconvenience of living without them."[6]

Eight of the first twelve presidents of the United States were slaveholders. Their view of the African remains etched in the Constitution until this day. Article I, Section 2 of the document states that a slave should be counted as three-fifths a human being.

Free labor helped build the infrastructure of the nation. America was largely an uncultivated wilderness. There were swamps to be drained. There were roads to be built. There were forests to be cleared and cities to be built. In the seventeenth century, America filled its labor needs with indentured servants. But in August of 1619, the crew of a Dutch ship made a fateful swap in Jamestown, Virginia. They left behind twenty black people in exchange for some unnamed goods. At first the legal status of the African in Virginia was uncertain at best.

Soon after their arrival, legislation defined the Africans as slaves for life.

Unlike the indentured servant, the slave had no rights, no legal recourse and no limit on the time of bondage. Laws were enacted which made anyone born of an African-American mother a slave for life. A slave could not simply flee the plantation and blend into the general population—his black skin would not allow that luxury.

Scientists created widely agreed upon theories concerning the Negro's biological inferiority. They placed him in a different genetic classification from white humanity. His capacity for learning and comprehension was said to be minimal at best. Preachers took up this cause from the pulpit on Sunday morning. For generations some of America's most noted theologians gave rationale to slavery in the United States. Their favorite exhortation to the slave was the apostle Paul's command, "Slaves, obey your masters."

American society looked to social scientists like John Locke, who wrote: "Every free man in Carolina shall have absolute power and authority over his negro slaves, of what religion or opinion whatsoever."

Second, in order to maintain the balance of power between master class and slave class, slaves must accept the theory of their own inferiority. Slaves must see white people as their betters. Blacks of any age were expected to show deference to the lowliest white person or even a white child.

Most slaves had a higher understanding of the nature of things. They had a complete grasp of the hopelessness of their situation. However, they sought to use it to their best advantage. Often they manipulated the master's belief in their inherent ignorance and docility to obtain advantages for themselves.

The Whip As a Means of Control

Only the crushing force of ruthless violence would make human beings submit. Early on the master class learned to wield the whip. The whip was the most common instrument of punishment. Almost every slave-master used it, and few slaves grew up without feeling its sting.

Methodist preacher Charles Wesley was shocked at the ghoulish treatment which he found administered to slaves in South Carolina. In 1736 he listened as slaveholders nonchalantly talked of punishments that would keep the slaves in line. One of the men offered, "First nail up a negro by the ears, then order him to be whipped in the severest manner, and then to have scalding water thrown over him, so that the poor creature could not stir for months after."

Slaves were whipped to encourage higher production rates in the fields. Poor work, stealing and running away could also be cause for a lashing. A whipping could leave ugly permanent scars on a bondsperson. Some slaves were whipped to death.

Ear cropping, branding and castration were also a part of the slave discipline. One Georgia plantation owner had a barrel with nails driven through it at all angles. He would put errant slaves in the barrel and then roll it down a hill. The slave who recalled this said, "When you got out you would be in a bad fix, but he didn't care. Sometimes he rolled the barrel in the river and drowned his slaves."[7]

Slaves got plenty of incentive to cooperate. One North Carolina plantation owner created a device he called "little hell." He dug a pit which he filled with burning coals. Sticks were laid across the coals. Black people who broke the rules were laid across that pit.

Mr. J. G. Baldwin witnessed the following scene at a public house near Halifax, North Carolina:

> A slave sat upon a bench in the barroom asleep. The master came in, seized a large horse whip, and without any warning or apparent provocation, laid it over the face and eyes of the slave. The master cursed, swore and swung his lash—the slave cowered and trembled, but said not a word. Upon inquiry the next morning, I ascertained that the only offence was to fall asleep, and this too in consequence of having been up nearly all the previous night, in attendance upon [his master's] company.

Blacks recalled how one slave owner named James Lucas "hung the best slave he had."[8] He caught him teaching other slaves to spell. An ex-slave named Henry Nix recalled what happened when his uncle was caught trying to read a stolen book. He said, "Marse Jasper had the white doctor take off my Uncle's fo' finger right down to the [first joint]."[9] Master Jasper did this as a warning to the others. Amputation of a finger was a common punishment for the crime of reading.

Corporal punishment was a mainstay of slavery until the South surrendered in the Civil War. One South Carolina slaveholder put it quite plainly: "[Blacks] can't be governed except with the whip."

5

....

Plantation Life

*T*he auction block was a place of weeping and gnashing of teeth. The destinies of thousands of African-Americans were decided there. It was the cornerstone of the institution of slavery.

Slaves might be shackled together in a long line called a "coffle" and marched over long distances. The hardships were beyond description. And the end of the line was the slave market.

In September 1834, English geographer George Featherstonaugh happened across a group of well-dressed white men who had camped out in the woods. The men laughed and joked, puffing on cigars in the cool of the morning. They were the drivers of a slave migrant party. Bought at auction, three hundred men, women and children were being taken to their new owner's mills to work. The twigs and hard ground had been their mattress; now they would walk all day. The whites rode in horse-drawn carriages and wagons.

Featherstonaugh watched as the black women and children warmed themselves by a fire. He recalled,

In front of them all, and prepared for the march, stood, in double files, about two hundred male slaves, manacled and chained to each other. I had never seen so revolting a sight before! Black men in fetters, torn from the lands where they were born . . . and driven by white men, with liberty and equality in their mouths, to a distant and unhealthy country, to perish in the sugar mills of Louisiana, where the duration of life for a sugar-mill slave does not exceed seven years![1]

Before a slave was put on the auction block, his or her value was estimated along with the rest of the master's livestock to be sold. Stephen Oates describes this ritual in his book *Fires of Jubilee.*

On the prescribed day, Nat and Cherry, Sam, Cary, Pete, Drew, Andrew, Violet, Jenny, Amy and all the children stood in line with the livestock: seventeen cows, eleven sheep, and 150 hogs. Then the white men with pens and ledger books moved down the line, examining slave and animal alike and assigning each a value.[2]

At the auction block, human beings were bid on like used furniture at an estate sale. Families were separated at the auction block, never to meet again on earth. Children were pried from the embraces of their hysterical mothers. Screaming and sobbing were part of the scene as husbands and wives were sold to different owners.

A slave woman might be purchased for breeding purposes. Her naked body was exposed on the auction block. Prospective buyers would knead her stomach to determine whether she could bear children. Some slave traders also specialized in what was known as "the fancy trade." They bought and sold women who were to be used as unpaid prostitutes.

A slave named John Thompson described the utter helplessness he felt in the face of a slave auction tragedy. He approached the slave trader as the procession was being lined up, his voice trembling with anger as he shouted, "For God's sake, have you bought my wife?"[3]

Indeed, the trader had purchased her. Thompson looked at his wife in chains and asked the trader what her crime had been. As it turned out, she had been sold simply because her master wanted money.

Perhaps the trader read daring and desperation on Thompson's face. He warned Thompson that he would be shot to death if he so much as went near the woman. John Thompson never saw his wife again. He later said, "I loved her as I loved my own life."[4]

The Slave at Work

Many slaves were leased out for work in cities and towns. They were trained as blacksmiths, artisans, carpenters, butchers and construction workers. Sometimes they were hired out to do dangerous jobs like laying railroad track. They also found duties as salespeople, domestics, typesetters and bookkeepers.

Plantation slaves often found themselves divided into two categories: house Negroes and field Negroes. Each of the positions had disadvantages and advantages. House slaves lived and worked in the "big house," the master's plantation mansion. The house slaves cooked the food, tended the children and cleaned the home. They served as butlers and maids. The handled the carriage-driving chores.

The house slaves usually had access to better food than the other slaves. They wore the master's and mistress's cast-off clothing. They most often lived in the big house with the master. Normally they slept on the floor, but sometimes they even slept in the same bed with their master and mistress, tending the bedroom fire during the night. The slaves were at the beck and call of the family, to wait on them hand and foot, night and day.

House slaves and field slaves were sometimes members of the same family. But distinctions were often placed between them by the masters: house slaves were seen as better than field slaves. For example, the Allston family house slaves in All Saints Parish, South Carolina, stated that they were "vastly superior to the ordinary run of the negroes, the aristocracy of the race."

House slaves lived in a precarious situation. They often found it difficult to relax, having to live at tiptoe stance in the master's shadow. During holiday times, when the field slaves could relax at night, guests would be visiting the plantation—and that meant extra work for the house slaves.

Field Negroes were housed in one-room wooden shacks with dirt floors. Often these homes offered little protection from the elements. One ex-slave complained, "The wind and rain will come in and the smoke will not go out." It was not unusual for several families to be crowded into one of these shabbily built huts.[5]

Austin Daniel recalled his Mississippi slave hovel.

[We] laid in bed many a night and looked through the cracks in the roof. Snow would come through there when it snowed and cover the bed covers. Before you make a fire [in] them days, you had to sweep out the snow so that it wouldn't melt up in the house and make a mess.[6]

Booker T. Washington recalled his childhood sleeping quarters: "We slept on a bundle of rags upon the dirt floor."[7]

Some slaves were fed in feeding troughs like horses or hogs. Hunger was a way of life. Said one slave, "I recollect seein' one biscuit crust, one mornin', dey throwed it out to the dogs, and I beat de dog to it."[8]

Ragged and often hungry, field slaves were usually expected in the field at the first ray of light. They toiled from dawn to dark, picking the crop under the watchful eye of a whip-wielding overseer. The overseer was often a poor white person employed by the master to carefully supervise the slaves' work. Slave drivers, enlisted from among the slaves, set the pace of work and were often charged with whipping slaves who did not keep up. The term "slave driver" is still with us today.

Slave Women

The female slave often worked alongside the men in the fields. However, her status was often even more precarious. Forced sex was common. Slaves were considered chattel who had no rights to their own bodies. They could not testify in court. There was no legal recourse that they could pursue to protect themselves. They lived solely by their master's mercy. Paul Escott wrote, "Some perverse individuals made slave men yield their place in bed and gave friends access to the women on the plantation."[9]

One slave owner named James Henry Hammond had sexual liaisons which produced children with several black women. Hammond, like so many other slave masters, used these children as slaves. However, he asked his white son Harry not to sell any of his children "or possible children" upon his death.

Slave Breeding

The legal importation of slaves into the United States was abolished long before slavery ended. To meet the ever-increasing demand for slave labor, owners bred African slaves like cattle or horses. Some owners kept a black man called a "stock man"—his function was to impregnate women. Sometimes the master would hire him out to other plantation lords who desired his reproductive services for their women. The stock man could father countless children whom he would never see.

One slave owner, James Roberts, kept fifty to sixty women whose sole purpose was breeding. It was estimated that these women bore twenty to seventy-five children a year. Roberts realized a handsome profit by selling off the children as soon as they could live apart from their mothers.[10]

A freed slave named Hannah Jones related the story of two men who became successful in the slave-breeding business. She said, "Ben Oil had a hundred niggers. He just raised niggers, on his plantation. . . . John Cross [Oil's brother-in-law] raised niggers too. He had a nigger farm."[11]

Slave Rebellions

The slaves' resistance to their plight came early in their struggle to survive in the United States. Slaves resisted by breaking tools; they challenged their masters by slowing down production. And sometimes they showed their anger in less subtle ways. Disgruntled slaves might burn their master's barn down. They quietly appropriated his livestock to supplement their woefully inadequate diets. Masters sometimes found themselves poisoned by trusted cooks.

Slaves ran away even from masters who considered themselves kind and benevolent. In April 1781, A British ship sailed up the Potomac and set anchor near George Washington's Mount Vernon estate. Eighteen of Washington's slaves fled from his property, choosing to take their chances with the British strangers.[12]

Slaves who ran away proved the greatest threat to the master's authority. Professional slave catchers, called "patrollers" (or "paddy-rollers" by the slaves), combed the back woods and swamps. They were aided by "negro dogs"—bloodhounds trained specifically for the task of hunting runaway slaves.

Some slaves remained defiant even in the face of capture. Frederick Douglass recalled one such slave. Douglass and several other men were cornered in a failed escape attempt. The patrollers aimed loaded pistols at the fugitive slaves. One slave hollered, "Shoot me, shoot me! You can't kill me but once. Shoot! Shoot! . . . I won't be tied."[13]

On August 28, 1783, the slaveholders' worst nightmare became a reality. A black man in the French colony of St. Domingue began to circulate a letter which read:

> Brothers and Friends:
> I am Toussaint L'Ouverture. My name is probably known to you. I
> have undertaken to avenge you. I want liberty and equality to reign
> through St. Domingue. I am working toward that end. Come and
> join me, brothers, and combat by our side for the same cause.[14]

St. Domingue was a wealthy island; it was certainly France's most
valuable colony. Its cocoa plantations raised sugar, coffee, cotton,
indigo, tobacco and cocoa. Its slave population outnumbered the whites
fifteen to one. L'Ouverture engineered a giant slave insurrection and
overran the military government.

When President George Washington caught news of the uprising, he
contacted Alexander Hamilton, secretary of the treasury. Under Washington's direction, $40,000 was sent to France to help squash the revolt.
The American tax money was lost as St. Domingue was conquered by the
ex-slaves. It was later renamed Haiti.[15]

News of the insurrection sent shock waves across the United States.
What would stop America's slaves from erupting in violence and
seeking their liberty? This was particularly troubling to states that
had large African-American populations.

Louisiana responded in panic. Governor Kerlerec ordered a ban on
the importation of slaves from the West Indies. The ban bankrupted
seven out of ten New Orleans citizens. Whites were terrified of a black
uprising. They responded by turning up the punishment pressure. A
slave named Caesar was whipped, then branded on the face, before his
wrists were cut and he was broken on the rack. Caesar's crime? It was
alleged that he had stolen a chicken, a pig and some clothes.

But even the most repressive tactics could not stop the yearning of the
human heart for freedom. Slaves still ran away. Often the other plantation
slaves would know where the newly liberated slave was hiding—but that
was a secret which they hid behind a façade of ignorance.

The Nat Turner Rebellion

On May 31, 1831, Joseph Travis woke up to find a mob in his
bedroom. They were dark-complexioned, mulatto and every shade
in between. Each had felt the sting of his lash. Travis shouted for
his wife. A field slave named Will made short work of Travis's life

with an ax, then did the same with his wife.

The slaves cut an angry swath of red through the cool Virginia night. They ignored all pleas for mercy. Only the shedding of blood would soothe their inconsolable rage.

Dozens of slaves joined the ranks of Reverend Nat Turner, the slave preacher who led this charge against the scourge of slavery. At each destination the body count rose. Even the women and children were killed. Only poor whites were spared. The slaves were stopped before they reached their destination: the munitions dump at Jerusalem, Virginia. Nat escaped the clutches of the state militia and eluded a massive manhunt. As the days went by, whites began to fear that Turner was somewhere plotting another uprising. But Nat Turner was eventually captured. He was unrepentant even as he faced the gallows. The preacher called out boldly, "Was not Jesus crucified?"[16]

A thick cloud of fear overshadowed the land in the wake of Turner's death. Whites grew terrified whenever they saw a group of blacks gathered in prayer. Great restrictions were placed on the black church.

In private the slaves sang a song about the departed preacher called "Ole Prophet Nat." The lyrics said, "You can't keep the world from turnin' round / Or Nat Turner from gaining ground."[17]

6

• •

Roots of the
Black Church

I magine that you are an African-American slave. The time is the mid-eighteenth century. Perhaps you live in New York City or Charleston, South Carolina. It is night. The day's work is done. You lie on your back assessing the incredible twists of history and geography that have brought you to this place, stripped away your name and transformed you into a living, breathing nonentity.

You are far from home. Gone is the material from which self-definition is woven. Friends, family and community are just hazy memories of life in another world. You were recently captured and brought here along with a lot of other black people. Most of them look like you, yet they speak another dialect. You cannot communicate with them. Your captors have given you a new name. They beat you if you do not answer to it. You work from dawn to dusk. Your back is sore. Your fingers ache. Your belly growls from hunger.

The warm African breezes that once whispered through your life are gone. It is December. It is cold—colder than you've ever imagined that it could be. You wake up the next morning to find the yard covered with a silky, white carpet. White flakes fall down from the heavens. What are they? No one can explain this to you. You stare into the heavens mesmerized. And you remember God.

The slave's understanding of the transcendent Creator was the only consistent hope in a world of disappointment. Slaves transposed symbols and figures from their indigenous religions to their understanding of the Christian faith. Some were taught the answer to the question, "Who is Jesus?" Many African Muslims adopted Christianity. Eventually the Christian faith was the instrument of social cohesion that helped instill a sense of community within the slave quarters.

Christianity in Africa

African men and women's first exposure to the Christian faith took place long before they first reached the shores of America. There is an old African proverb that is still repeated to this day. It says, "When the white man came to Africa, they had the Bible and we had the land. Now we have the Bible and they have the land." Christianity existed and even thrived in some areas of West Africa during the fifteenth century. Christian missionaries sometimes used the faith to pave the way for interests of a more commercial nature.

In 1489 Behemoi, the leader of the Wolof people, was converted and baptized in Senegambia, West Africa.[1] In 1491 several chiefs were baptized in Sierra Leone. The king of Benin, Nigeria, also came to profess faith in Jesus Christ.[2]

In 1491 Mani Sogno, a noble from the Congo, became a Christian.[3] He even had a church built there. Emmanuel, the king of the Congo, accepted the faith and Christianity became the dominant religion in that country. The Catholic Church at Rome began to appoint bishops to serve in the Congo.[4] Wherever European slave industrialists settled in Africa, churches were established. The Christian church was in West Africa for a century before the first black slave picked up a hoe in America. It is not beyond the realm of imagination to suppose that a number of black Christians were chained to the bottoms of slave vessels and transported to the Americas.

A Cross for African-Americans

By the eighteenth century, Christian missionaries began to evangelize the Native American and African populations of the United States. The Society for the Propagation of the Gospel in Foreign Parts was established in London. Bishop Porter published a tract detailing the spiritual impetus behind the mission. He wrote, "Despicable as they are in the eyes of man, they, nevertheless, the creatures of God."[5]

Missionaries from several different denominations preached the gospel to slaves in both the North and the South. But quite often these missionaries also held African people in the bitterness of chains. Their messages often consisted of wooden admonitions to obey Master and to avoid theft. Hellfire was promised to belligerent slaves.

Whites preached about Christian brotherhood during the Sunday morning devotional services. On many plantations the slaves accompanied their masters to church. They were relegated to the back pews in the house of the Lord—or to a balcony constructed with the darker believer in mind. It was called "the Negro Gallery." (Some whites referred to it as "nigger heaven.") This seating area was suspended high above the rear of the church. The white membership usually preferred that their chattel be neither seen nor heard.

Remarkably, the slaves' religious experience was similar in a number of diverse places. Slaves had little contact beyond a carefully defined circle of fellow bondspeople. They knew very little of life beyond the confines of the plantation or city home in which they labored. Yet a vocal, rhythm-oriented worship style emerged in most areas where blacks were allowed to worship.

The Underground Church

The sweet aroma of Southern pine trees softly scented the cool night air. Crickets chirped amidst the hooting of the owls. The music of the forest was interrupted only by the uneven thud of coarse, calloused feet as they broke twigs. The soft footfalls belonged to slaves.

In the distance the master's dogs howled. The baying of the hounds was a constant reminder of what awaited the slaves should the master become wise to their whereabouts. These African-Americans were defying all the conventions of the institution of slavery. They were absent from the house of bondage without permission. If caught they could be severely whipped.

In a clearing by the lake the assembly gathered. Hands that had picked tobacco or cotton beneath the sun clapped in rhythm beneath the stars. A young child led in singing "What a Friend We Have in Jesus." Some of the words were altered from the original copyrighted version. New choruses and verses were included at random.

A young woman in a red-and-white gingham dress erupted in ecstatic utterances. "Oh, Jesus, have mercy, Lord," she pleaded. She began to dance a slow pirouette to nonexistent music. Her dance turned into a ballet—a poetic expression of collective suffering. An elderly voice behind her urged, "Let the Lord have his way, child."

An old slave with chronically bloodshot eyes burst into song. "When Israel was in Egypt land . . ." His voice failed in the lower registers, defying every recognizable key. But no one cared. The hymn resonated from the deep pain down in his soul. His coarse cotton shirt covered the age-old scars on his back. The congregation joined him: "Tell old Pharaoh, let my people go."

The preacher could not read. It was not allowed. Using a great deal of ingenuity, he constructed a sermon from a rambling collage of colorful snippets that he had managed to pirate from the plantation's sanctioned services. He was often convincing in his exegesis. The power of the singing and preaching stirred the embers of faith in the hearts of the downtrodden congregants. Perhaps it was in the stolen moments of a nighttime meeting that the answer to the question "Who is Jesus?" became clear to the slaves.

Black and Christian

Stifled by the constraints of sanctioned services, Southern slaves often formed their own praise and worship services. One former slave recalled, "When de niggers go round singing 'Steal Away to Jesus' dey mean dere gwine be a 'ligious meetin' at night. De masters . . . didn't like dem 'ligious meetins, so us natcherly slips off at night, down in the bottoms or somewhere. Sometimes us sing and pray all night."[6]

The "ring shout" was originated during these covert, unsanctioned services. Bishop Daniels, a renowned African Methodist Episcopal preacher, visited a Southern brush service after the close of slavery. He recalled, "After the sermon they formed a ring and with their coats off, sung, clapped hands and stomped their feet in ridiculous heathen's way." Daniels asked the pastor to call a halt to these worship expressions. The bishop recalled, "They remained, singing and rocking their bodies to and fro."[7]

This type of spiritual witness troubled the stalwarts of the slavocracy. Some realized that the Christian faith in the wrong hands could collapse the delicate social structure. If slaves ever came to believe that God loved blacks and whites equally, they would become even more difficult to keep in their place. As a result, some slaveholders did not allow their slaves to get near the teachings of the Bible. Gus Clark recalled such a master. He said, "My Boss didn't 'low us to go to church, er to pray er to sing. Iffen he ketched us praying or singin' he whipped us. . . . He didn't care for nuthin' but farmin'."[8]

Eli Johnson's master was furious about Johnson's desire to host unsanctioned prayer services. He threatened to give Johnson five hundred lashes if he caught him with his head bowed in an illegal worship gathering. To the master's great chagrin, faith had bolstered courage and resolve within Johnson. He replied, "In the name of God, why is it, that I can't after working hard all week have a Saturday evening? I'll suffer the flesh to be dragged off my bones . . . for the sake of my blessed Redeemer."[9]

The Ministers in Master's House
The Christian experience berthed an enemy right under the master's roof. The black preacher was dangerous to the house of bondage. He infused the slave with a concoction that was poison to the slavocracy. It was called "hope."

Beyond earshot of the master and mistress, the slave preacher taught from the Exodus narrative. He recalled how a man named Moses followed the leading of God into the heart of a slaveholding territory named Egypt. The slaves shivered as the preacher imitated God's voice and cried, "Tell ole Pharaoh to let my people go!" They howled as the Red Sea opened up again in their imaginations. They could almost feel the foamy waves cover their feet as the walls of water came crashing down on the forces of Egypt. If God heard the groaning of the Hebrew children, would he not hear the cries of his children in America?

Gabriel Prosser made his home on the outskirts of Richmond, Virginia. He was a twenty-five-year-old student of the Bible. Prosser identified strongly with one of Israel's judges. He so revered Samson that he grew his hair long like the biblical figure. Like Samson, Prosser believed that he had been destined by God to deliver his people from tyranny and oppression.[10]

In 1800 Prosser planned to lead a slave revolt of astronomical proportions. His slave army would kill any white person who stood in their path. Their objective was to seize the arsenal at Richmond. They would also raid the state treasury. Ultimately, Prosser and his legions desired to set up a separate African-American state within the borders of the United States. Ten to fifteen thousand slaves kept the secret until the eve of the revolution. But two of them told their master. Prosser was executed.[11]

Denmark Vesey was a Methodist Christian. He attended the Hampstead Church in Charleston, South Carolina. Vesey organized and planned a massive slave insurrection in 1822. His coconspirators included several Sunday-school teachers and at least one preacher. Two house slaves gave him away before the revolution was to begin. It was estimated that somewhere between three and nine thousand slaves were awaiting Vesey's order.[12]

Across the South, black church gatherings became strictly regulated. Two or three gathered in Christ's name could spell danger. The July 1, 1857, edition of the Tuskegee (Alabama) *Republican* argued, "Preaching by Negroes ought to be utterly abolished. Negro preachers are invariably the corrupters of slaves, and they are the head of all this mischief that is brewed among them."[13]

The Black Church Comes Above Ground

George Liele was born the property of Henry Sharpe in 1750. Sharpe moved his family and slaves to Burke County, Virginia. New surroundings bought a change in Master Sharpe's life. In Georgia he became active in the local church. He was even given the post of the deacon. His slave George Liele also converted to the Christian faith and was baptized. Together with a slave named Andrew Bryant, George Liele founded the First African Baptist Church of Savannah, Georgia.[14]

Henry Sharpe permitted his slaves to build a church building where blacks could worship God. Andrew Bryant was given full ordination as a Baptist clergyperson.

Local whites both hated and feared Reverend Andrew Bryant. They sought to make things difficult for him and his parishioners. Slave patrols whipped slaves on their way to church, even if they had the proper authorization from their masters. Some of the church members were arrested on their way to the house of prayer.

The law finally caught with Andrew Bryant and his brother Sampson. They were both arrested and tortured for their faith in Christ. It was said that they were "inhumanely cut and their backs were so lacerated that their blood ran down the earth as they with uplifted hands cried unto the Lord." At the height of the beating, Rev. Bryant said that he "rejoiced not only to be whipped but to suffer death for the cause of Jesus Christ."[15]

The First African Baptist Church went on to become black America's first "megachurch," with seven hundred members.

The Black Church Is Born in Struggle

One Sunday morning in 1794, Richard Allen and Absalom Jones knelt down to pray in the segregated Negro gallery of St. George's Episcopal Church in Philadelphia, Pennsylvania. Allen, a former slave, had purchased his freedom. He was a licensed Methodist exhorter. He was certainly no stranger to the pulpit at St. George's Episcopal Church. From time to time, he was called upon to deliver the Sunday morning sermon.

On this particular morning, the meditative moment was interrupted by a soft but insistent voice. Absalom Jones was being summoned by a deacon whom Allen later identified only as H.M. The deacon commanded, "You must get up—you must not kneel there."[16]

Jones had somehow knelt down in the "whites only" section of the segregated church. He sought but a moment to complete his prayer before he retired to the black section. "No," H.M. growled, "you must get up now or I'll call for aid and force you away!"[17]

Absalom Jones ignored him and continued to petition his God. His prayers were interrupted again. H.M. and a church trustee grabbed him. The three of them wrestled right there in the sanctuary. H.M. and the trustee succeeded in pulling Jones from his knees.

A crowd of outraged African-Americans walked out of St. George's Episcopal Church en masse. Richard Allen recalled, "All went out of the church in a body . . . and they were no more plagued with us in that church."[18]

On July 17, 1794, Absalom Jones became the first black Episcopal priest in the United States of America. He founded and served as the pastor of Philadelphia's St. Thomas African Episcopal Church. Richard Allen went on to found the African Methodist Episcopal (A.M.E.) denomination. He pastored the Mother Bethel A.M.E. church in Philadelphia. A.M.E. churches opened their doors all over the United States, the Caribbean and Africa. Together Jones and Allen headed up the Free African Society, which provided benevolent services to the city's black community. All over America black worshipers followed their lead. Black-led churches were founded across denominational lines.

The Great Awakening

A tremendous time of spiritual renewal and revival landed on the shores of America in the eighteenth century. It was known to many as "The Great Awakening." Preachers like Englishman George Whitefield infused the gospel message with an intense passion and fervor. Whitefield was an oratorical genius who did not limit his message to an otherworldly religion.

In 1740 Whitefield castigated slave lords for treating their people like "horses" and "dogs." "The blood of them spilt for your respective providences will ascend up to heaven against you," he prophesied.[19] Reverend Whitefield insisted that blacks be allowed religious education.

Ironically, Whitefield had a change of conscience. In the 1750s he became an avid supporter of the very institution that he had once publicly denounced. Reverend Whitefield became a plantation baron, a slave owner. He used his considerable influence to persuade Georgia trustees to allow slavery into the new colony. Rev. Whitefield rea-soned, "The trade will be carried on whether I will [it] or not; I should think myself highly favored if I could purchase a number of slaves."[20]

Benjamin Lay was a Quaker layperson who abhorred the institution of slavery. The cruel treatment of the black captives galled him. He found that Northern slaveholders could be particularly cruel. Some of them would refuse to spend money on shoes for their slaves even in the snowy dead of winter.

One afternoon Lay came into a Quaker meeting with an object lesson. He walked in with a book in his hand that resembled the Bible. Unknown to his fellow worshipers, he had hollowed out the inside of the book and implanted a bladder filled with red juice. In a moment of high drama, Lay stood up and cried out, "Oh Negro masters, who are contentedly holding your fellow creatures in a sate of slavery . . . it would be as justified in the sight of the Almighty . . . if you should trust a sword through their hearts as I do this book!"[21]

Men and women screamed in terror as a red substance resembling blood came showering out of the book. Lay was immediately ejected from the fellowship. But eventually the English Quakers pressured their American brethren to reject human bondage. Quakers who persisted in their slaveholding ways could no longer make policy decisions within the denomination. The antislavery voice became very prominent within the Quaker community. Runaway slaves could often find shelter in Quaker households.

Christianity and the Antislavery Debate

The debate concerning slavery often raged from the pulpit. Reverend Isaac T. Tichenon, pastor of the First Baptist Church of Montgomery, Alabama, had the honor of addressing the general assembly of his home state on the topic of slavery. He said, "[That] slavery is sanctioned by the Bible seems scarcely to be of doubt. Founded upon the divine decree, Canaan shall be servant of servants unto his brethren; existing in the days of the patriarchs, twice spoken of in the Ten Commandments with laws written in the New Testament for its regulation, it stands as an institution of God."[22]

Amos Dresser, a student at Lane Seminary in Ohio, journeyed to Tennessee in the summer of 1835. His aim was to sell Bibles so that he could pay his seminary tuition. Somehow the hapless student found himself arrested and charged with being an abolitionist. He was given twenty lashes. The vigilance committee, which ordered him whipped, was composed of several prominent local Christians. One of the elders had served Dresser communion just a few days before his whipping![23]

The August, Georgia, *Chronicle* commented, "He [Dresser] should have been hung high as Haman, to rot upon the gibbet, until the wind whistled through his bones. The cry of the whole South should be *instant death* to the abolitionist where he is caught."[24]

Abolitionists

Abolitionists did not scare easily. They were vocal enemies of the slavocracy. Abolitionists were a diverse lot. They were often treated like outcasts by the larger society. They were white, black, male and female. They used any means at their disposal to upset the racist social order.

An editorial in the *New York Express* sought to dissuade the clergy from entering the antislavery fray. It said,

> What have you to do, revered gentlemen, with slaves more than your great master had when he and his apostles lived among slaves . . . . Why thus pervert your business, your salaries, into political machinations when the whole country is steeped in sin,

personal individual sin, and demands your conversion of the sin of the individual not of states? The *souls* of men, not States of men, is your vocation. Mind your business, then, and let other people mind theirs.[25]

An editorial in the *National Anti-Slavery Standard,* an abolitionist newspaper, responded,

Can any advice be better than this? Can any be more respectful to ministers of the gospel than to advise them to 'enjoy their salaries'? It is as if we should say, What is the first duty of a clergyman? To draw his salary! What is his second duty? To enjoy it. . . . Do the sins of the world trouble him? Let him draw his salary! Is his congregation forward! There is a balm at the bankers! . . . We never heard of more than one of [the disciples] who received any salary at all, and so far from enjoying it, he kept enough to buy a rope, with which he hanged himself.[26]

The New Freedom Fighters

William Lloyd Garrison came into the world struggling. He was born in Newbury Park, Massachusetts, in 1805. At an early age his rabble-rousing father abandoned Walter, his mother and his four siblings to swim through whiskey glasses in the local gin mills. At age thirteen Garrison landed a job at a local newspaper. By the time he was sixteen, the newspaper was printing his articles—anonymously. By age twenty-one he owned his own newspaper, *The Free Press.*[27]

Garrison, who was white, believed in nonviolent protest against the institution of slavery. He rose up to become a powerful voice in the abolitionist movement. Garrison addressed the matter at an 1838 abolitionist convention in Boston. He said, "We believe that the penal code of an eye for an eye and a tooth for a tooth has been abrogated by Jesus Christ and that, under the new covenant, the forgiveness instead of the punishment of enemies has been enjoined upon his disciples in all cases whatsoever."[28]

Death threats seemed only to bolster Garrison's resolve. One night a mob broke into a house crying, "Garrison, Garrison! We must have Garrison!" They placed a rope around his neck as the mayor of Boston pleaded for Garrison's life.[29] He survived that episode to become the editor of the first abolitionist newspaper, *The Liberator.*

Frederick Douglass

A black man pressed through a crowd one day to shake William Lloyd Garrison's hand. Though the two were complete strangers at the time, the man felt compelled to speak with Garrison. Frederick Douglass was impressed with a speech that Garrison had just given. Sanguine brown eyes peered out from beneath a thick forest of jet black hair. A stern but appreciative smile broke through his handsomely chiseled visage.

He said, "These ministers who define slavery from the Bible are of their 'father the devil.' And those churches that regard slaveholders as Christians are synagogues of Satan. In fact, Mr. Garrison," he concluded, "our nation is a nation of liars." Strong words from a black man at the height of slavery and antiblack terrorism.[30]

Frederick Douglass preached the horrors of slavery from firsthand experience. He himself had been a fugitive, looking over his shoulder and sleeping with one eye open. His mother had been sold to another plantation when he was young. He saw her but a few times in life. His father was rumored to have been his white master. He never knew his real age, a fact which troubled him until his death. (Such knowledge was often withheld from slaves.)

Douglass served a master who was a sadist. He recalled being awakened at dawn by his aunt's piercing screams. The master had hung her up by the wrists and was whipping her. She was covered in blood. Douglass reflected, "The louder she screamed, the harder he whipped, and where the blood ran fastest, there he whipped the longest. He would whip her to make her scream and whip her to make her hush."[31]

Frederick was sent to labor in Baltimore, Maryland. There his master's wife taught him how to read the Bible. Thomas Auld, his master, was furious. He yelled, "If you give a nigger an inch he'll take an ell; he should be taught nothing but the will of his master and learn to obey it." Auld believed that "learning would spoil the best nigger in the world." He warned his wife, "If you teach that nigger how to read the Bible, there will be no keeping him."[32]

Auld was almost entirely correct. The knowledge that Douglass gained made slavery intolerable to him. He fell under the classification of a "bad nigger." This meant that he was sullen, defiant and openly discontented. The cure for "bad niggers" was an extended stay at the residence of a professional "nigger breaker." Thomas Covey was a staunch Methodist. He was chosen for the task. Douglass was delivered to his tutelage in January 1833. Covey enlisted Frederick Douglass's singing voice to lead the hymns at the family's nightly devotional services.

One day Thomas Covey approached his young charge, intending to beat him. He was about to receive the surprise of his life. Frederick Douglass later explained, "I resolved to fight: and suiting myself to the resolution I seized Covey by the throat."[33]

When it was over, Douglass stared into Covey's blackened eyes, bloody nose and swelling lips. A sense of pride welled up in him. A fighter was born. From that time on Douglass said, "I did not hesitate to let it be known of me, that the white man who expected to succeed in whipping me must also succeed in killing me."[34] Eventually he escaped north and to freedom.

John Brown's Rebellion

John Brown was a devout Christian who devoured Scripture passages with a passion. He was noted for his uncanny ability to commit long passages of the Bible to memory. Brown was a Kansas-born Caucasian. When he was a young man working as a cattle herder, a landlord welcomed him into his home. A sight which he witnessed in the man's backyard appalled him.

There in the cold was a half-naked black boy. While the landowner and his guests basked in the warmth of a glowing fireplace, the child slept exposed in the yard. John Brown saw the boy beaten with an iron shovel for some minor grievance. Brown became deeply concerned about the plight of the slaves. He began to ask himself, "Is God their Father?"[35]

Years later, his band of antislavery fighters was approached by a black man whose family was about to be sold away. He pleaded for John Brown's help. Brown and his men freed the man and his family, as well as some other blacks. They made a run for it.

The slave's owner eventually stumbled across Brown's hideout. One of Brown's men invited the slaveholder inside the house and then asked, "Do you want to see your slaves?" When the man answered in the affirmative, the abolitionist produced a double-barrel shotgun and pointed it in his face, saying, "Well, just look up the barrels and see if you can find them." The slaveholder pleaded for his life. He was released unharmed, minus his slaves. However, Brown and his men were not apostles of nonviolence.

The governor of Kansas sent a telegram to a local law enforcement officer. It said, "Capture John Brown, dead or alive."[36]

The marshal responded, "If I try to capture John Brown, it'll be dead and I'll be the one that'll be dead."[37]

John Brown formulated a plan to free a massive number of slaves in Virginia. He wanted to capture the munitions dump at Harper's Ferry. Brown believed that many slaves and poor whites would come to his struggle. They would all flee to the mountains and there create a free community for the African-American people.

Harriet Tubman had welcomed Brown into her home. However, she was ill and not able to join him in his venture. Frederick Douglass was also enlisted early on in the planning stages of the small-scale war. He saw it as impractical. A friend who had accompanied him to a meeting with Brown told him, "I believe I'll go wid de old man."[38]

An observer noted, "In John Brown's house and in John Brown's presence men from widely different parts of the continent met and united into one company, wherein no hateful prejudice dared intrude its ugly self—no ghost of distinction found space to enter."[39]

On Sunday morning, October 16, 1859, John Brown's men met for prayer. There were twenty-one of them in all. Sixteen were white and five were black. Two of the band were Brown's own sons. That morning after Bible study, they left to deliver America from the curse of African-American slavery.

John Brown's raid on Harper's Ferry failed. There was a massive bloodletting. The two sons who had accompanied him were killed. From his jail cell Brown wrote, "Christ the great captain of liberty; as well as of salvation; and who began his mission as foretold by him; by proclaiming it, saw fit to take from me the sword of steel after I had carried it for a time but he has put another sword in my hand."[40] He was referring to the sword of the Spirit.

A Quaker woman wrote to Brown in prison, "If Moses led out the thousands of Jewish slaves from their bondage . . . then surely, by the same reasoning, we may judge thee a deliverer who wished to release millions from a more cruel oppression." She reasoned that if George Washington was crowned a hero for challenging British taxation, Brown should be afforded even more adulation for his efforts to free the slaves."[41]

Unfortunately, the courts did not see it that way. John Brown was sentenced to death by hanging. There was a famous picture painted of Brown on the way to the gallows. It portrays a tall white man with a long, unruly white beard. A uniformed military escort surrounds him. A black woman stops the procession to raise her child up before John Brown. Brown reaches over to kiss the child.

John Brown's willingness to die for African-American freedom escalated the abolition argument all over the United States.

The Fugitive Slave Bill

On September 18, 1850, President Millard P. Fillmore signed the Fugitive Slave Bill into law. Southerners whose slaves had escaped to Northern free states could now demand their return. No person of African descent was safe as long as there was still an open market for their lives somewhere in the United States.

The slave catchers were notorious in their dealings. Dr. John Doy told the story of a "yellow man" brought into the Elatte County jail in handcuffs by a slave trader. The man exclaimed hysterically that he was indeed a free man. The trader reached into the man's shirt and extracted a tin case which contained manumission papers. Doy said, "[He] took out the papers which proved that the man was entitled to his freedom, read them, tore them up and threw them into the stove. And that man was driven off South that very night with a large gang of slaves."[42]

The Underground Railroad

The Underground Railroad was one of the most radical methods of abolition. It was a carefully devised network of homes that provided passage and safe haven to slaves in their escape from bondage. Railroad "conductors" would shelter escaped slaves in their basements or secret rooms. They would transport them across state lines. They would supply them with fresh clothes and money.

Harriet Tubman was the shadow that lingered in the brush behind the slave quarters. She traveled at night, leading bands of slaves northward via the Underground Railroad. Her calling code was a traditional African-American hymn called "Promised Land."

Tubman's Promised Land was not as far as heaven, but the slaves found it almost as inviting. When the bondspeople heard the song, it was their cue to escape. An elaborate network of safe houses had been established to hide runaways day by day as they worked their way north to freedom. Slaves found homes in Philadelphia, New York and other cities. Many times the Promised Land was Canada where the Fugitive Slave Law could not be enforced.

Secret signals, escape tunnels and disguises were all a part of the Underground Railroad. Most slaves who escaped did so without any such aid. However, thousands found freedom through this system.

Reverend Henry Highland Garnet was a "conductor" on the Underground Railroad. He was the son of escaped slaves. He was installed as the pastor of Liberty Street Presbyterian Church in Troy, New York, in 1843. Garnet opened his parsonage as a sanctuary for runaway slaves.

During a speech called "Address to the Slaves of the United States of America," Garnet said, "Brethren, the time has come when you must act for yourselves. . . . There is not much hope of redemption without the shedding of blood. If you must bleed, let it all come at once—rather die freemen, than live to be slaves."[43]

Garnet's words were prophetic. Bloodshed was coming. The battlefields of America would soon be soaked in the blood of its young men. But the slaves would be free.

7

· ·

Civil War Divides the Union

*H*istory often remembers Abraham Lincoln as the bearded angel of liberation. He has long been touted as the freedom fighter who gallantly broke the African-American's shackles of slavery. Frederick Douglass was the black community's premier spokesperson of the nineteenth century. He had quite different recollection. Douglass said:

> He was preeminently the white man's President, entirely devoted to the welfare of white men. He was ready to deny, postpone and sacrifice the rights of humanity in the colored people to promote the welfare of white people in this country. . . . We are at best only his step-children.[1]

Abraham Lincoln was born in Hardin County, Kentucky. He shared that tract of land with 1,627 white males and 1,007 African-American slaves. Lincoln's great uncle Isaac owned scores of slaves. His Uncle Mordecai also held human stock. His mother's guardian had been a slave owner.[2]

Lincoln himself proved to be very much of a man of his times. During his presidency, he argued for gradual emancipation of America's slave population. He suggested that the government offer financial remuneration to the slave masters after their chattel were freed. He was also in favor of sending blacks to Haiti and to Liberia, West Africa. He poured large sums of government money into projects which did just that.

President Lincoln once told an African-American delegation:

> You and we are different races. We have a broader difference than exists between any other two races. Whether it is right or wrong I need not discuss, but this physical difference is a great disadvantage to us both, as I think your race suffer very greatly, many of them by living among us, while ours suffer from your presence. ... If this is admitted, it stands to reason at least why we should be separated.[3]

On December 20, 1860, something happened that would distinguish Abraham Lindoln's presidency in the annals of American history. The state of South Carolina seceded from the United States of America. Lincoln had yet to be sworn into office.

Many Southern political leaders misread Mr. Lincoln. They believed that he would demand that the south divest itself of slavery. Perhaps they should have paid closer attention to his inaugural address. There he stated, "I have no purpose directly or indirectly to interfere with the institution of slavery where it exists. I have no lawful right to do so and no inclination to do so."[4]

Lincoln was, however, very much concerned about the spread of slavery in the western territories. Northerners realized that the South would have economic control of these territories if slavery were allowed to exist in them. Enterprising Northerners would be left with no chance to compete against gangs of forced laborers. The matter had been an issue of grave debate for years. However, when the southern states seceded from the Union, the argument escalated. Lincoln and his force went to war to reunite a nation.

Blacks in Flight

As Union forces encroached upon southern plantations, huge numbers of slaves would run away in search of sanctuary. Sometimes these former slaves would outnumber the Union regiments. Union troops called them "contraband." They were considered property confiscated from citizens in rebellion. Often they were men but sometimes these escaped bands consisted of whole families. A *New York Times* correspondent observed the inside of a "contraband" camp. In December of 1862 she wrote a story called "Freedom in the Abstract."

"What shall we do with them?" the story began. "Along with our forces on the return, came some three hundred Negroes of all ages, sexes, color, sizes and conditions. Trumping eagerly through the deep mud came old paralytic women, bent with age. . . . Mothers waded through mud and water, carrying babies in their arms sustained by the thought that they had at length obtained the wonderful blessing of freedom. . . . Barefoot children, ragged adults, young women clad in hermaphrodite suits of half petticoats and pantaloons grinning over the sublime thought that they had obtained the priceless boon—Freedom."

The correspondent reported that ten to twenty slaves died from abuse in one day at camp. She concluded, "Freedom in the abstract is a fine thing, and will do to fight, preach, pray, suffer, starve for; but when Freedom amounts to no more than what Negroes obtain (at the camp) it is a different affair."[5]

General John C. Fremont of the Union army created the first emancipation order. On August 30, 1861, General Freemont ordered rebel slaves in Missouri freed. Lincoln exploded when the news reached him. He saw great ramifications which could result from Fremont's impetuous order. Kentucky, Delaware, West Virginia and Maryland were slave states which had opted to fight with Lincoln to save the Union. Lincoln did not want to antagonize them by bringing the issue of slave freedom to the war agenda.

General Fremont would not be swayed from his course. He refused to rescind the order without a direct command from Abraham Lincoln himself. On September 11, 1861, Lincoln gave him just that order.[6]

Abolitionists were quite vocal in response to Lincoln's desire to evade the slavery issue. The president answered his critics:

> My paramount object in this struggle is to save the Union, and is not either to save or to destroy slavery. If I could save the Union without freeing any slave, I would do it, and if I could save it by freeing all the slaves, I would do it; and if I could save it by freeing some and leaving others alone, I would also do that. What I do about slavery and the colored race, I do because I believe it helps save this Union.[7]

Black People with Guns

Still the slaves kept coming. Southern planters tried on many occasions to move their slaves deeper into confederate territory to avoid the approaching Yankees. Some sold their slaves to the Deep South.

Two hundred thousand blacks joined the armed forces of the Union. Black women worked as nurses in its hospitals. Black men toted the army's supplies and cooked its food. However, white soldiers did not want to fight alongside of African-American troops. Corporal Felix Branigan of the New York 74th declared, "We are a too superior race for that."[8]

Ohio's governor, David Tod, was approached by abolitionist John Mercer Langston. Langston suggested that the state could fill its quota of soldiers simply by allowing blacks to don the blue uniform of the Union. Tod snarled, "Do you not know, Mr. Langston, that this is a white man's government; that white men are able to defend and protect it? When we want colored men, we will notify you."[9]

The war was not going well. The Union needed more troops to wage a successful campaign. Frederick Douglass was incensed at the Union's reluctance to arm its African-American citizens. He understood that Blacks would be able to parlay their battlefield endeavors into future freedom. He also reasoned that if blacks shed blood for America, they might later have been accepted as full citizens. He stated: "This is no time to fight only with your white hand and allow your black hand to remain behind you."[10]

The idea of putting guns in the hands of ex-slaves and then sending them to the battlefield to face their former masters was a radical one. However, the Union was facing desperate times. In July of 1862 the Union forces put guns in the hands of black men.

The African-American troops proved both competent and fearless in battle. Robert Smalls, an African-American, commandeered a Confederate vessel and sailed it to Union waters. Harriet Tubman acted as a spy for the Union forces. She led several forays behind enemy lines.

The donning of the blue uniform did not in itself signal the end of racial discrimination. Blacks faced torture and reenslavement if captured. Blacks were given the most dangerous assignments and were equipped with obsolete weapons. The standard pay for white soldiers was $13.00 a month. The new African-American freedom fighters received only $10.00 a month.[11]

The Emancipation Proclamation

In September 1862 Abraham Lincoln signed the Emancipation Proclamation. The document said nothing about blacks held as slaves in
Union states. It did however manumit the slaves of the Confederacy.
According to one writer, "Lincoln slowly began to agree with those who
thought that the fastest way to break the South's resistance and end
the war would be to free the slaves." Emancipation was slated for
January 1, 1863.

On the evening of December 31, 1862, Boston's Tremont Temple was
packed with anxious African-Americans. They listened impatiently as
William Wells Brown, Anna E. Dickerson, J. Sella Martin, Leonard A.
Grimes and Frederick Douglass gave speeches. Finally a messenger
raced toward the platform yelling, "It's coming! It's on the wires."[12]

A second messenger followed him down the aisle swinging a telegram in his hand. The church went up in a euphoric shout even before
it was read. Pandemonium broke out. Eventually Frederick Douglass
began to sing the hymn, "Blow Ye the Trumpet." Lincoln's signature
had freed the slaves.[13]

True, Lincoln's proclamation freed only slaves who were in bondage
in rebel territories. However, full emancipation could not be far away.
The Union needed the full cooperation of the African-American soldiers. It became increasingly clear to President Lincoln that a huge
complement of "colored" troops could turn the tide of the war.

Lincoln feared that if he did not emancipate those who fought for
his cause, they might cease to war for him. On August 19, 1864, Lincoln
wrote, "Abandon all the posts now possessed by black men, surrender
all these advantages to the enemy, and we would be compelled to
abandon the war in 3 weeks. . . . Freedom has given us the control of
200,000 able-bodied men, born and raised on Southern soil. It will give
us more yet."[14]

The War's End

The body count rose to terrifying levels. There were sixty thousand
dead or wounded at Gettysburg alone. Atlanta was on fire. Gray-coated
young men were falling on the battlefields. The Confederacy became
a lost cause. There was even talk of arming the slaves and sending
them out to fight against the Union—but this idea never caught on.

On April 9, 1865, General Robert E. Lee surrendered his sword at the Appomattox courthouse. The South was finished.

Some ex-slave owners were furious over the news that their slaves would be emancipated. A Spartansburg, South Carolina, man wrote in his journal, "[All of the] negroes leave today, to hunt themselves a new home, while we will be left to wait upon ourselves."[15] One Texas slaveholder was devastated by the news that slavery was over. He fell into a state of depression and then psychosis. A year later he committed suicide.[16]

The war was over, and so was American slavery. Some slaveholders tried to keep their chattel in bondage by withholding the news from them. The mistress of a Camden, South Carolina, plantation would not allow her slaves to leave, informing them "it was not at all certain that they would get freed."[17]

But they *were* freed. Ex-slaves often changed their names after the Emancipation Proclamation was announced. Slave marriages were formalized. (Slaves had not been allowed to be legally united in matrimony.) And people traveled—for the sheer joy of going from one place to another unrestricted, and to see the breadth of the land and the wonders of God's creation.

The black man was free at last. Or was he?

*   *   *

Slavery lasted for generations and centuries. It became the foundation of black-white relations in America. Lincoln freed the slaves because he needed their labor and firepower to defeat the confederacy. But America would not be prepared to deal with four million freed slaves as they tried to claim their freedom.

Part Three

• •

From Reconstruction to the New Black Leadership

At the height of the Civil War, President Lincoln signed the Emancipation Proclamation. It served to free only the slaves held in Confederate territories. It said nothing about Africans held in Union slaveholding states such as Kentucky, Maryland, Delaware and West Virginia. However, the end of the war did come to mean complete abolition. As the South sank down in tatters, a mighty shout rang out in the slave quarters. Slavery was dead.

Blacks marched in parades. They left plantations where they had lived for generations. Freedom promised a new life in America—an existence that one hardly dared dream of. But all was not well. Slavery's ugly twin sister, segregation, came of age in the wake of the South's fall.

Once black people were sold like horses or crows in the Wall Street area of New York City. They served in such diverse places as Massachusetts and Rhode Island. Slave pens were erected on the banks of the Raritan River at Perth Amboy, New Jersey. However, most Northern states abolished the institution in the decades that preceded the Civil War. When slaveholding ended in the North, a system of racial customs was put in place that relegated black people to what Malcolm

X would later call "second-class citizenship." Rigid segregation governed race relations. Southerners adopted these same codes at the end of American slavery. The system of racial caste was known as Jim Crow. And Jim Crow was African-America's new enemy.

However, the black church proved to be an ally in the freedom struggle. A host of African-American leaders rose to lead black people in the fight for justice. In part three we will read of some of them.

8

· ·

Reconstruction

*E*mancipation. The sons and daughters of West Africa sent up a collective cry that reverberated from one end of the United States to the other. They danced, they paraded, they toasted, they cried. Freedom had come at last.

The end of the Civil war brought changes in the traditional relationships between blacks and whites. One Virginia coach driver really became caught up in the spirit of things. When the Union soldiers informed him that he was free, he marched straight through the front door of the big house uninvited. He went upstairs into his former master's bedroom. Once there, he proceeded to pick out his choice of clothes from his master's wardrobe. After he had properly attired himself in a suit, he chose a matching watch and chain set. Then he turned to his dazed ex-master and informed him that in the future he would have to drive his own coach.[1]

A former bondsman happened to see his former master in the custody of the authorities. The man had fallen from plantation aristocrat to war prisoner. The victorious former slave greeted his former enslaver with the words, "Hell, Massa, bottom rail top dis time!"[2]

One white gentleman greeted an older African-American man with a disparaging phrase, "Hello, uncle!" The newly freed man snapped, "Call me mister!"[3]

Southern whites hated the sight of black soldiers who returned toting firearms. They were a symbol of Southern defeat. It was a new day.

When the shouts of joy had died away there were some realities to face. The slaves had been manumitted largely without any financial resources. Most slave owners did not share any of the economic rewards that they had derived from the slaves' back-breaking labors. There were few jobs for the freed blacks. Many masters had released their slaves penniless to a hostile world. Rivers of bitterness churned in their bellies as they watched their human revenue walk away.

Forty Acres and a Mule

During the Civil War, General Sherman of the Union army granted half a million acres of land to freed slaves in Georgia, South Carolina and Florida. This act was known as Special Order 15. All over the South, African-American people held out hope that they would be awarded the promised forty acres and a mule. Rumor had it that the land giveaway would be officially announced on January 1, 1866.

A bill passed in March 1865 had laid the groundwork for the Bureau of Refugees, Freedmen and Abandoned Lands. It became commonly known as the "Freedmen's Bureau." The agency gave aid to poor whites and newly freed blacks. The bureau was authorized to lease land to chosen designees in increments of up to forty acres. This land was the confiscated property of the defeated Confederate land barons. But to the surprise of many, President Johnson sided with these former owners. He gave their land back to them when they swore allegiance to the Union.

Blacks in Beauford, South Carolina, picked their guns up again and fought off the federal troops who had come to displace them. In October 1865 President Johnson sent General Howard, executive officer of the Freedmen's Bureau, to South Carolina to quiet them down. Howard was extremely dismayed at the subterfuge and betrayal. A huge assembly had been called on Edisto Island to make the announcement that the blacks would have to relinquish their new properties. A woman began the proceedings with a soulful rendition of "Nobody Knows The Trouble I've Seen." General Howard wept as he looked into a sea of black faces and regretfully informed them that they would have to relinquish their land to their former slave owners.[4]

One man cried out, "Why General Howard, why do you take our

lands? You take them from us who are true, always true to the government! You give them to our enemies. This is not right."[5]

In January 1867, a battalion of federal troops confronted a posse of angry black settlers in South Carolina. The soldiers had their orders. They were to order the African-Americans away from the land. The property would then revert to the ownership of its pre-Civil War owner. There was one thing that they had not counted on. The blacks showed up armed to the teeth. They promised to walk through the jaws of death before they gave up their land. One of the leaders said, "We have but one master now—Jesus Christ—and He'll never collect taxes or drive us off." To that another leader yelled, "Fall in, guards!" The blacks assumed battle position. The soldiers turned around and marched off.

It didn't take long for the ex-slaves to find out that freedom was not something that could be legislated. Economic clout and political power were the things that spelled freedom in a capitalist democracy.

President Johnson and the African-American

Frederick Douglass knew that he had trouble on his hands following the untimely death of President Abraham Lincoln. It was the slightest of nuances that had tipped Douglass off concerning the vice president's racial sensibilities. From a seat at the inaugural ball, Frederick Douglass observed Johnson interacting with Abraham Lincoln. Johnson pointed at the great African-American leader and frowned. Douglass told a dinner companion, "Whatever Andrew Johnson may be, he is certainly no friend of our race."[6]

Andrew Johnson was an ex-slave holder. In his annual message given on December 3, 1867, President Johnson attributed America's success as a nation to the "glory of white men." He said, "Blacks have shown less capacity for government than any other race of people. . . . No independent government has ever been successful in their hands. On the contrary, whenever they have been left to their own devices they have shown a constant tendency to revert to barbarism. . . . Of all the dangers which our nation has yet encountered, none are equal to those which must result from the success of the effort now moving to Africanize the half of our country."[7]

Frederick Douglass led a delegation to Washington to speak with Johnson about black enfranchisement. After he left, the President of the United States exploded, "Those [multiple expletives] thought they had me in a trap! I know that [expletive] Douglass, he's just like any nigger, and he would sooner cut a white man's throat than not!"[8] Johnson was adjusting the thermostat for the political climate of the country.

The New Black Codes

Between 1865 and 1866, Southern states began to pass legislation called "black codes." These laws forbid slaves to vote, run for office or carry firearms. There were regulations concerning the congregation of African-Americans after dark.

These laws were inspired by a desire to recreate the pre-emancipation social arrangement between blacks and whites. In Mississippi black children whose parents were unable to provide for them were returned to the care of their former masters.[9]

The black codes in Texas required railroad companies to attach a separate car in which blacks had to ride. Some communities imposed curfews on their black citizens. African-American preachers were often refused the liberty to preach the gospel without a recognized license.

Landless and broke, the ex-slaves soon found themselves again at the mercy of their ex-masters. A sharecropping system was instituted. The plantation owner gave the ex-slave a piece of land, a shack, seed and tools. In exchange, the African-American family mortgaged their lives to him. They eked out a tiny subsistence, often living in perpetual debt—sometimes to the very man who had once owned them.

Special taxes were levied against blacks only. Those who couldn't pay were incarcerated. Sometimes a white patron would pay the tax in return for labor on his plantation. Strict vagrancy laws were enacted, laws that affected blacks inordinately. Among the "criminals" listed were "able-bodied males over eighteen years who are without means of support and remain in idleness." Often a strong captive labor base was created by jobless ex-slaves trapped in violation of the labor laws.[10] These black men were made to work on chain gangs or contracted to white planters.

The Search for Education

The newly freed African-Americans craved something that had been denied them for centuries. They longed to learn how to read. After slavery ended in the South, schools were created for the African-

American populace. Many of the institutions of higher learning were financed by the Freedmen's Bureau. Northern Christian churches set up independent societies to help the freed slaves in their quest for knowledge. Missionaries from the Northern states went South to teach the newly freed blacks the mysteries of the written word. Black preachers taught God's Word and the written word. Often the Bible and the Farmer's almanac were their first textbooks.

Blacks put pennies and nickels together to raise extraordinary sums of money for educational purposes. They contributed to institutions like Howard University and Hampton Institute (now Hampton University).

The New Black Church

After the Civil War, African-American families emptied the Negro galleries and black pews of the white churches. They purchased buildings and worshiped God in the style that suited them. Whereas the white churches had almost exclusively segregated blacks from leadership positions, these new churches were black-owned and black-led. The role of the African-American church began to evolve spiritually, socially and politically. The church became the center of the African-American community. It was the place where blacks could lay down the façade that had become a survival mechanism in the other world. They could laugh at their own brand of humor. Since they were barred from playhouses and pageants, the church became the place where they could wear their finest clothes. Community news was passed along at the church. Young people met and married within its walls. Attendance and participation were very high.

The role of the African-American pastor began to evolve as well. One white Baptist preacher remarked, "[The black preacher's] influence is far above any man of color in the country." Rev. Shady W. Jones was an A.M.E. Zion preacher with political ambitions. He ran for a congressional seat in 1868 but lost. The Tuscaloosa *Independent Monitor* labeled Rev. Jones "the greatest rascal among the Negroes of Tuscaloosa," recommending that he be "Ku Kluxed and Negro ambition squelched in its incipiency." Rev. Americus Trumblies was murdered in 1871 because, whites said, "he was exerting an influence upon the colored population that was deleterious."[11]

African-Americans Gain the Ballot Box

On June 13, 1866, the United States Congress passed the Fourteenth Amendment. It overrode the infamous Black Codes. The Civil Rights Act of 1875 gave African Americans the right to the ballot box. Blacks began to register to vote in America for the first time. Juries were integrated in the South for the first time. Black politicians were voted into office.

Black Progress

Against incredible odds, some blacks experienced tremendous prosperity during the Reconstruction and afterward. Some blacks who had been free before the war were able to hang on to their wealth. Some owned tremendous real estate holdings, stocks, bonds or businesses.

A Crescent City land speculator named Thomy Lafon increased his financial holdings by speculating in swampland during the Union occupation. He used his wealth to contribute heavily to black charities.

A mulatto elite class developed in the black community. Some school districts refused teachers who were not light-complexioned. Sometimes these blacks had white relatives who helped them obtain educational opportunities.

The Civil Rights Act of 1875 gave African-Americans the right to pursue justice against whites who misused them. Some whites, angry that blacks had been given the ballot, refused to vote. Black political muscle flexed as the Republicans began to demand a public school system that would educate blacks. Juries began to be integrated in the South for the first time.

A wealthy South Carolinian complained, "If a negro should sustain any ill feelings against a white man and can muster the slightest shadow of a case against him, he rushes off immediately to Beaufort [the county seat] and there he finds a ready and willing mill to grind the respectable portion of the community to ashes."

New Voices in Politics

Blacks served at every level of government during Reconstruction. There were black ambassadors, U.S. treasury agents, grand jurors and mail agents. African-Americans served as secretaries of state, customs agents and U.S. marshals. A black man named Jonathan J. Wright of

South Carolina was elected to the position of associate justice of the Supreme Court in 1870. This is mind-boggling when we consider that slavery had been a thriving institution within that state just five years previous to his elevation to that office!

From 1869 to 1870 James W. B. Bland represented Virginia in the United States Senate. Blanche K. Bruce of Mississippi was the first African-American to serve a full term as a United States senator. He served from 1875 to 1881.

Norris Wright Cuney was one of eight children, born in 1846 to a confederate general and a slave woman. He served as the collector of customs in Galveston, Texas, from 1889 to 1893. From 1884 to 1896, Cuney served as the Republican national committeeman for Texas. This position was the highest political office in the state.

In 1872 Lt. Governor Pickney B. S. Pinchback became the first black governor in the United States. The country would not have another one until the end of the twentieth century. In 1873-1874 Pinchback became the only person in the history of the United state to simultaneously claim seats in the U.S. House and Senate. However, he was denied these seats when election impropriety charges were introduced. He spoke out strongly for African-American enfranchisement and protested for greater educational opportunities for blacks. He once said, "Wealth is the great lever that moves the earth."

Jeremiah Haralson was born a slave in 1846. In 1874 he was elected to Congress. He became the leader of a Republican delegation at the national convention of 1876. One Alabama newspaper decried him for being "black as the ace of spades."

Martin Delaney is called "the father of Black Nationalism." He once said that African-Americans are "a nation with a nation." In the coming years Marcus Garvey, Malcolm X and many other would pick up this theme. Delaney had worked carefully with colonization efforts which repatriated freed slaves to the shores of West Africa. He published the first African-American newspaper, the *Mystery*. Delaney later went to work with Frederick Douglass' newspaper, *The North Star*.

In 1850 Delaney entered Harvard Medical School only to be expelled for his protest of a racial incident. During Reconstruction he served as a jury commissioner and trial justice in Charleston, South Carolina.

The Ku Klux Klan

In 1877 the federal peacekeeping forces were called back from the Southern states. The South was left to work out its racial problems by itself. Whites and blacks were both afraid. Whites feared bloodshed and insurrection from disgruntled blacks. They also feared losing political power to blacks, who were the majority population in many voting precincts. Blacks feared the backlash of now-poor whites whose way of life had forever changed due to the Civil War. The editor of one Southern newspaper wrote: "We must either render this the white man's government or convert the land into the Negro's cemetery." The Ku Klux Klan set out to do both.

Pulaski, Georgia, was a sedate little Southern town located eight miles south of Nashville, Tennessee. This unassuming hamlet unleashed one of the most fearsome terrorist organizations ever to be birthed from the bowels of the United States. The Ku Klux Klan was originally chartered as a social club in 1865. However, its name soon became synonymous with the lynching rope.

The name *Klan* struck terror into the hearts of Southern blacks. The white-robed avengers of white supremacy rode most often at night. The white they wore symbolized racial purity. Red "drops of blood" sewn on the robes symbolized a willingness to shed their own blood for the cause. However, the blood shed was rarely their own.

The klansmen and klanswomen wore masks. Underneath were the faces of shopkeepers, law enforcement officials, saloon owners and other average citizens. The smiling baker during the day could easily be the masked man who rode at night. Blacks who refused to conform to the subservient Southern way could expect an unfriendly visit from the Klan's welcome committee. The Klan visitor's kit came complete with a flaming cross and hangman's rope.

If the Klan had an "at risk" list, black preachers were often at its top. They were often the only blacks who could live completely independent of white support—no one could make them obey by threatening their livelihood. And black clergy served as the civic leadership of the community.

The Ku Klux Klan decreed that the ministry of the gospel should not be proclaimed by any African-American in Goshen Hill Township, South Carolina. Reverend Lewis Thompson defied their orders. Once his intention to preach became known, he received a letter in the mail.

His brother said: "It was a wide paper with a mark in the shape of a coffin, and in the mark was 'Lewis Thompson, if you preach any more.' The Three K's—Kill, Kill, Kill, it was taken to mean . . ." The note went on to say, "You are not to preach here; a colored man is not to preach in this township."[12]

Thompson thought it more important to obey God than man. Like the apostle Paul, he was willing to preach the gospel even as death loomed dangerously real. Reverend Lewis Thompson, itinerant preacher of the gospel, was indeed martyred. The organization that refers to itself as the "Christian Knights of the Ku Klux Klan" took his life and then threw his body in a river. They prevented his family from giving him a decent burial.

The Civil Rights Act of 1875 was eventually rescinded as unconstitutional. Black politicians were sent home in droves. History seemed to be moving backward. And yet the embers of hope still burned within the African-American community.

9

. . . .

The Rise of the New African-American Leaders

*P*ost-Reconstruction freedom was a tenuous thing for African-Americans. In 1896 the Supreme Court decided a landmark case known as *Plessy vs. Ferguson.*[1] The country's highest legislative body gave sanction to the "separate but equal" doctrine that solidified racial segregation in public accommodations. The court argued that it was "powerless to eradicate racial instincts."

Racism was legally defensible in post-Reconstruction America. Still many blacks were able to find their place in American life. One example is Lewis Latimer, born in 1848, who became the only black member of Thomas Alva Edison's research team.[2] He aided in the development of the light bulb. Latimer also worked closely with telephone pioneer Alexander Graham Bell. Garret Augustus Moran is credited with the invention of both the traffic signal and the gas mask. For most blacks, however, job opportunities were limited.[3]

African-Americans needed visionaries to light the dark nights of hopelessness. They needed fighters who would put life and limb on the line for an elusive thing called "freedom." And new leaders did emerge.

A great number of them would be found courageous, creative and competent. Others would leave the black community arguing over their tactics long after they were gone.

Ida B. Wells

A train chugged noisily along the winding country roads of Tennessee. A young black woman named Ida B. Wells sat admiring nature's beauty from a comfortable coach seat. The train conductor interrupted her quiet moment. He informed the schoolteacher that she was seated in the ladies' car of the train. He suggested that she remove herself to the "colored only" train car.[4]

Ms. Wells later recalled, "He tried to drag me out of the seat, but the moment he caught hold my arm, I fastened my teeth in the back of his hand." It took three men to pry her out of the train car. Not one to walk away from a fight, Wells enlisted the services of a lawyer. It was not long before the newspaper headlines read, "Darky Damsel Gets Damages." The court awarded her $500 in damages.[5]

Wells was quite outspoken, so much so that she was forced to carry a pistol with her. She said if the situation arose she would be forced to "sell my life as dearly as possible." But she would do much of her future fighting with a fountain pen.

Her insights, written under the pseudonym "Iola," appeared in newspapers across the country. Her columns often featured details of lynchings and other race crimes afflicting blacks in the South. In 1889 she bought a one-third share in a newspaper called the *Free Speech*.

Local white citizens became incensed at an article suggesting that many charges of rape by white women against black men were actually consensual sexual encounters. On May 27, 1892, the offices of the *Free Speech* were trashed and the business manager run out of town. An article in the *Commercial Appeal* read, "The black wretch who had written that foul lie should be tied to a stake at the corner of Main and Madison Streets, a pair of tailor's shears used on him, and he should then be burned at the stake."[6]

Ida B. Wells was in New York at the time of the incident. At the frantic urging of friends she decided to stay there. Thomas Fortune, the editor of the *New York Age,* invited her to join his newspaper as a writer. She later bought a share in the paper. For the rest of her life she continued to be a champion of the African-American cause and a spokesperson for women's suffrage.

Mary McLeod Bethune

Mary McLeod was another very resourceful Southern black woman. Her blazing eyes and prominent chin belonged to a person of strong will and unquenchable determination. She was born to a poor family in Mayesville, South Carolina, on July 10, 1875.[7] As a teenager she was granted a scholarship to Moody Bible Institute where she was trained to be a missionary. She decided against the foreign field, reasoning that she could best use her gifts and talents to aid her people here in America.

On October 4, 1904, Miss McLeod opened the doors of the Daytona Normal and Industrial Institute for Girls. She turned to the African-American community for financial support for the school.[8] Neighbors fried up batches of deep-battered chicken and sold dinners to benefit the school. Fishermen donated the catch of the day to the students and their instructor. Orange growers donated a portion of their crop to finance the fledgling institution.

In less than two years the school's enrollment rose from 5 pupils to 250. Daytona's mission encompassed the entire community. Mary McLeod set up missions for poverty-stricken children in neighboring communities. She headed a fund drive to build a hospital, which she named after her mother. She married, and her name became Mary McLeod Bethune.

Many students probably remembered her most for something that happened the evening before Daytona's 1920 election day. That fateful evening some surprise guests stalked around the grounds of the school. Their evening wear consisted of white sheets and pointed hoods. Their calling card was a fiery cross. Like many whites, the Klan was unhappy with Mary's outspoken support of opposing candidates in the forthcoming elections.

When the students saw the parade coming toward the building, they were terrified. Undoubtedly some had visions of the robed knights storming the building. In the midst of the screaming and chaos, Mary stood her ground and said, "Don't be afraid of the Klan! Quit running! Hold your head high, look them straight in the eye, and make no apology to anyone because of color. When you see a burning cross, remember the Son of God, who bore the heaviest cross of all." She stood and began to quote passages from the book of Psalms. Then she led the petrified young ladies in the hymn, "God Will Take Care of You."[9]

The klansmen paraded up the drive of the school, but Mary refused to be intimidated. The next day she was back at the helm of the voter registration drive.

The name of the school was later changed to Bethune Cookman College. Mrs. McLeod Bethune went on to head the National Association for Colored Women. In 1935 she won the NAACP's prestigious Spingarn medal.

Booker T. Washington

One afternoon a young man arrived at the Hampton Institute in Virginia seeking enrollment. He shifted nervously from one foot to the other. He was ragged and dirty. His pockets were empty except for some small change. Born a slave, he had never known his birth date. He had to make up his own last name. Booker T. Washington had not long ago arrived from a five-hundred-mile trek, most of it on foot.[10]

Months before, Washington had overheard some men talking in the coal mine where he was employed. They were discussing a place almost beyond the realm of his imagination. They spoke of the Hampton Institute, a school of higher learning for African-American people. If such a place truly existed, Booker T. knew that he must go there.

Now, after a series of tribulations that would have made Job quit, he was inside the door at Hampton. He waited patiently in the waiting area. Student after student was enrolled, and finally the head teacher turned to him. "The adjoining recitation room needs sweeping. Take the broom and sweep it." As it turned out, this was Booker T. Washington's admission exam into the Hampton Institute.[11]

From this humble start he would rise to receive dinner invitations from the president of the United States and the queen of England. Booker T. Washington was one of the most powerful black leaders that America has ever known.

After graduating from Hampton, Washington founded the Tuskegee Institute in Tuskegee, Alabama, as a higher-education facility for African-Americans.

George Washington Carver, the famed scientist, joined Washington's teaching staff in 1896. He headed the school's agricultural department. Carver was a genius who developed an amazing number of foods and other products from the peanut. He created peanut milk. He made Worcestershire sauce from peanuts. He could make products like ink and facial cream from peanuts.[12] George Washington Carver brought prestige and media attention to Tuskegee Institute.

Washington's fame continued to rise. A speech that he delivered at the Atlanta Exposition cemented his place in history. As the governor of Georgia looked on, Washington explained his views on black progress in the nineteenth century: "Ignorant and inexperienced, it is not strange that in the first years of our new life we began at the top instead of the bottom; that a seat in Congress or the state legislature was more sought than real estate or industrial skill. . . . It is at the bottom of life we must begin, not at the top. Nor should we permit our grievances to overshadow our opportunities."[13]

W. E. B. DuBois

Not all African-Americans saw eye to eye with Mr. Washington. One of his staunchest critics was a mulatto gentleman, short of stature, who hailed from Barrington, Massachusetts. His name was W. E. B. DuBois.

DuBois called Washington's meteoric rise to the seat of black leadership "easily the most striking thing in the history of the African Negro since 1876."[14] DuBois steamed, "Mr. Washington's program practically accepts the alleged inferiority of the Negro races."[15]

DuBois was the first black person to receive a Ph.D. from Harvard. He was a social critic and prolific writer who sought to make reason of black people's existence in America. He spoke a "double consciousness" that the black person is forever made to wrestle with. DuBois diagnosed it this way: "One ever feels his twoness, an American, a Negro, two souls, two thoughts, two unreconciled strivings in one dark body whose dogged strength alone keeps it from being torn asunder."[16]

In his book *Dark Waters*, DuBois prays, "Forgive us, good Lord, we know not what we say! Bewildered we are and passion tossed, mad with the madness of a mobbed and mocked and wounded people. Straining at the armposts of thy throne, we raise our shackled hands and charge thee: God, by the bones of our stolen fathers, by the tears of our mothers, by the very blood of the crucified Christ; what meaneth this? Tell us the plan; give us the sign!"[17]

W. E. B. DuBois predicted that the problem of the twentieth century would be the color line.[18]

The Founding of the NAACP

In 1903 DuBois called upon a group of prominent African-Americans to meet with him in Canada. They called themselves "The Niagara Movement." Their goal was to form an organization that would address the racism that threatened the black community in the United States.

In 1906 a young white social worker came to the Niagara Movement's annual meeting at Harper's Ferry, Virginia. Mrs. Mary Ovington, a settlement worker in the slums of New York City, was horrified at the living conditions of black people in the South.

She later met with several prominent whites to head a new civil rights organization. They called it the National Association for the Advancement of Colored People or NAACP. One of those who signed the original charter was DuBois.

In 1910 a Jewish Columbia University professor named J. E. Springarn was elected to the leadership of the NAACP. DuBois was eventually named editor of the association's newsletter, *The Crisis.*

In 1916 James Weldon was awarded the position of field secretary and national organizer for the NAACP. He was a man of many talents. Johnson was a poet, who composed works like "God's Trombones." He was the songwriter who composed the Negro national anthem, "Lift Every Voice and Sing." He wrote the groundbreaking novel *Autobiography of an Ex-Colored Man.*

Walter White became the assistant secretary of the NAACP in 1910. He wrote: "I am a Negro. My skin is white, my eyes are blue, my hair is blond. The traits of my race are no where visible upon me."[19]

White's light complexion allowed him to gather first-hand coverage of lynchings and other race crimes. Often he stood a hair's breadth from the lynching fire, his African heritage undetected.

Walter White's secret was released somehow during a 1919 race riot in Elaine, Arkansas. He was urged to make a run for it. White took the first train out. The conductor said, "Mister, you're leaving just as the real fun is starting. There's a [expletive] yellow nigger down there passing for white, and the boys are going to get him now. When they get through with that nigger, he won't be passing for white any more."[20]

The Great Migration

A great African-American exodus from the Southern states started in the late nineteenth century. Between the years 1889 and 1910 the black population of New York quadrupled. Other Northern cities experienced the same phenomenon. Between 1915 and 1916 a boll weevil infestation ruined the cotton crop and caused a depression in the South. Even more African-Americans came north seeking work. Industries placed ads in the black newspapers offering jobs in the North—ads that attracted African-Americans to the promise of higher wages.[21]

The new African-American refugees were segregated in Northern ghettoes. Many immigrant groups—Irish, Polish, Italian and others—had started out here. Later they found a way to leave their sweltering ghettoes and be assimilated into the American mainstream. Blacks would be denied this privilege. They were barred from trade unions and hired largely for the most strenuous and dangerous of menial jobs.

Even middle-class blacks were segregated into the slums. Prostitution, gambling and alcohol were readily available forms of escapism.

Blacks in the Military

In 1917 the United States declared war on Germany. The Marines and the Coast Guard barred blacks from enlisting in their ranks. But African-American volunteers flooded Army induction centers. NAACP and student protesters prevailed and the Army lifted its ban against black officers. Yet an overwhelming number of the blacks who served in Europe unloaded ships, built military installations and moved supplies.

The 93rd division of the 369th infantry was composed completely of blacks. They were among the few who actually engaged the Germany army during the war. The Germans nicknamed these African-American soldiers "the hellfighters." They once kept the Germans under fire for a record-breaking period of time. They were the first Allied unit to cross the Rhine into Germany.

One hundred seventy-one of the men of the 93rd division were decorated. One of them, Private Henry Johnson, of Albany, New York, found himself surrounded by enemy German soldiers. In what became known as the "battle of Henry Johnson," he killed twenty-four of them. Johnson and another soldier named Needham Roberts were from Harlem's 369th infantry. They were the first African-American soldiers to receive France's coveted Croix de Guerre medal.[22]

But racism was still alive and well. In the summer of 1917 the third battalion of the army's 24th infantry was stationed at the Logan army base a few miles from Houston, Texas. The black soldiers bristled at the segregation laws which restricted their access to public accommodations. They began to defy the local statutes. They angrily tore down "white only" signs. They sat in the "whites only" section of the movie theatre. They reportedly said, "We're from New York and we'll sit where we please. We're as good as any white man in town."[23]

A. Philip Randolph

Harlem, New York, became the unofficial capital of African America in the early twentieth century. A. Philip Randolph arrived in the sprawling village in 1911. The son of an A.M.E. minister, he was born in Crescent City, Florida, on August 5, 1889, and named after the Old Testament king Asa. Randolph founded the first black socialist political club in Harlem's 21st Assembly District. Along with friend and cofounder Chandler Owen, he launched a radical African-American newspaper called *The Messenger.*

The plight of the Brotherhood of Sleeping Car Porters came to Randolph's attention. Editorials about their union began to appear in *The Messenger.* The porters earned a bare subsistence wage and were generally ill-treated. They were forced to demean themselves by doing the buck and wing dance on the train platforms for extra tip money to augment their meager earnings. They were also forced to work unpaid excursions.

Randolph became embroiled in a life-and-death struggle for the recognition of the Brotherhood of Sleeping Car Porters. Meetings were held in alleys and on street corners to avoid spies. Sleeping-car porters were fired by the score as their membership in the fledgling union became known. It took twelve years of struggle before the union was officially recognized by the AFL-CIO.[24]

But times were changing. New voices could be heard in places like Harlem. Blacks were redefining the image of the African-American through the arts. Writers like Zora Neale Hurston, Countee Cullen, Paul Lawrence Dunbar, Cane Toomer, Langston Hughes and others were gaining national recognition as poets and authors. These new black writers created a new literary school of creativity with its own criteria. Artists such as Albert Motley recreated black life on canvas. This movement has been called the Harlem Renaissance.

Marcus Garvey

In 1916 a heavy-set black man with a thick moustache stood on a Lenox

Avenue street corner and preached a message of black nationalism to passersby. He was West Indian; in fact, he had just recently arrived from Jamaica. He had originally come to the States to garner support for a proposed Jamaican version of Booker T. Washington's Tuskegee Institute. A reporter for the *Panama American* newspaper wrote, "He would probably pass unnoticed in a crowd until he speaks. He has the most precious of bounties, the gift of speech."[25]

Marcus Moziah Garvey was born on August 17, 1887, in St. Ann's Bay, Jamaica. He rose from that Harlem street corner to become the leader of the largest black organization ever. The membership of the Universal Negro Improvement Association (UNIA) became worldwide in scope. The circulation of the *Negro World,* its newspaper, was between 60,000 and 200,000.[26]

Garvey once asked, "Where is the black man's government? Where is his king and his ambassador, his army, his navy, his men of big affairs?" When he could not find them, Garvey proposed to create them. He was a nationalist who believed that black people should control their own destinies. He scoffed at black leaders like DuBois who relied on white dollars to support their efforts. Garvey's message was one of black self-reliance. He often called upon black people to take pride in their ancestral roots.

In 1920 the Universal Negro Improvement Association sponsored a great convention. Delegates came to Harlem from twenty-five countries. Thousands cheered the pageantry of the parade that marched down Lenox Avenue, through the heart of the community. Marcus Garvey's troops marched that day in full regalia. There were the Black Cross nurses dressed entirely in white. There was the African Legion in their dark blue uniforms, swords swinging at their sides. That night 25,000 people jammed into Madison Square Garden to hear their leader proclaim, "Up, you mighty race. You can accomplish what you will!"[27]

That night Garvey announced the launching of the Black Star Line: a commercial shipping company that would sponsor cruises as well as do hauling. Shares in the Black Star Line were sold only to people of African descent.

The Beginning of Woes for the UNIA
Marcus Garvey may have been a motivator without peer, but he was a poor businessman. His biographer, E. David Cronon, writes, "In the

selection of his associates Garvey was more interested in unquestioning personal loyalty than in business competence."[28] Too often he did not get either. The ships he purchased turned out to be both grossly overpriced and barely seaworthy. His ill-fated business endeavors made him vulnerable to government scrutiny.

Marcus Garvey made a major miscalculation on June 25, 1922. He paid a visit to Ed Clarke a high ranking official in the Knights of the Ku Klux Klan. The Klan was the most visible symbol of white intolerance in American society. Many blacks saw Garvey's visit as collusion with the enemy.[29]

Marcus Garvey was never at a loss to defend himself. He said that the Klan was not just an organization but the very "spirit of America."[30] He argued, "There is absolutely no hope for equality, politically, socially and economically within the bonds of the United States of America so long as a white man is alive."[31] W. E. B. DuBois said, "Marcus Garvey is without a doubt the most dangerous enemy of the Negro race in America and in the world. He is either a lunatic or a traitor."

A. Philip Randolph joined the "Garvey Must Go!" campaign. In 1922 Randolph received a package in the mail. To his great chagrin he found that the box contained a human hand! An attached note said, "If you are not in favor with your own race movement, you can't be with ours. . . . We have sent you a sample of our good work. Watch your step or else."

The senders said, "[We want] to see your name in your nigger improvement association as a member, paid up too, in about a week from now." They warned, "Be careful how you publish this letter in your magazine or we may have to send your hand to someone else." The package originated from New Orleans, Louisiana. It was signed, "Ku Klux Klan."

The UNIA began to crumble from within. Reverend James W. Eason of Philadelphia, Pennsylvania, almost came to blows with Garvey on the stage of the 1922 convention. Eason left the organization to preach his perceived shortcomings of the UNIA. He was leaving a New Orleans, Louisiana, church after one such lecture. Three men opened fire on him and left him crumpled in the street. Before he died, Reverend Eason identified two of the men as Universal Negro Improvement Association members.[32]

Marcus Garvey was convicted of mail fraud stemming from the mismanagement of the Black Star Line. He wrote from an Atlanta penitentiary:

If I die in Atlanta my work shall only begin . . . but I shall live, in the physical or spiritual to see the day of Africa's glory. When I am dead wrap the mantle of the Red, Black and Green [the black liberation flag] around me, for in the new life I shall rise from God's grace and blessing to lead the millions up the heights of triumph with the colors you know. Look for me in the whirlwind or the storm, look for me all around you, for with God's grace, I shall come and bring with me countless millions of black slaves who died in America and the West Indies and the millions in Africa to aid you in the fight for Liberty, Freedom and Life.[33]

In 1927 Marcus Garvey was released from prison and banished from the United States. He died on June 10, 1940, in London, England, at age fifty-three. Today he is remembered by millions and crowned with something approaching sainthood for his message of black pride and unity. His birthday is celebrated as a holiday in the West Indian community.

* * *

The fight for inclusion in American life was a long and frustrating one for African-Americans. The repeal of the Civil Rights Act of 1875 sent most of the new black political leaders home. Blacks in the South continued to be denied voting rights and full participation in the American society. It would take a groundswell of protest across the nation before the civil rights of black people would become a reality in America.

Part Four

•••

From the Civil Rights Movement to the Black Power Revolution

*I*n the late 1930s millions of African-Americans sat in their living rooms, glued to their radios. The boxing matches were being broadcast. Joe Louis lifted them out of their seats with his powerful lefts and rights. He was their champion—a black man. He was humble: in the end he would say, "Just another lucky night. I'm glad I won." When he won, all of black America rejoiced.

In 1947 Jackie Robinson was the first black person to be drafted from the segregated Negro baseball leagues to the formerly segregated major leagues. Robinson opened the doors for blacks who came after him.

In 1954 Thurgood Marshall and the NAACP legal defense team were opening up doors of another kind. They led the fight against segregated schools. The battle went all the way to the Supreme Court. Segregated schools were ruled "inherently unequal" and were outlawed by the nation's highest court. This was just one of many victories accomplished by the NAACP which changed the quality of life for people of color in America.

By the late 1950s rock 'n' roll began to come of age. African-American artists like Chuck Berry and Little Richard were often banned from radio play. Black rock 'n' roll was known as "race music" until a young white man named Elvis Presley learned to approximate it and was named its king.

As we have seen, African-Americans had worked for generations to achieve equal opportunity in America. In 1955 some citizens from a small city in Alabama would take that fight to another level.

10

. . . .

The Civil Rights Movement

*O*n the evening of December 1, 1955, strange gossip filterd throught the streets of Mongomery, Alabama. It was said that a black woman named Rosa Parks had been dragged off the Cleveland Avenue bus in handcuffs. Her fellow passengers sat by muted and helpless as two burly policemaen forced her from the rear of the crowded vehicle. Rosa Parks was a law-abiding, churchgoing lady. She was arrested for defying the segregated seating arrangement that had been mandated for all public vehicles in Montgomery, Alabama.

You could hear talk of what happened to Mrs. Parks in the barbershop on South Jackson Street, in the teacher's lounge at Public School No. 1 and in various Montgomery barrooms. Often such talk was whispered. Montgomery's people of color were afraid, and there was much to be afraid of. The African-American who dared to challenge the segregation statutes could wind up dangling from the business end of a rope. The Ku Klux Klan did their level best to protect "the Southern way." In most cases, they were successful.

Jim Crow
The legal segregation system called "Jim Crow" rested on presuppositions born of slavery. The belief that blacks were essentially childlike,

docile creatures in need of paternalistic care had been nurtured over generations. From the minstrel shows to the movies, blacks were always pictured as pickaninnies, lazy but lovable morons, or domineering, unattractive mammies.

Blacks and whites were separated at water fountains and rest room facilities by signs that read "colored" or "white." Housing was segregated. Churches were segregated. Even the prisons and the graveyards were segregated. In many ways, Montgomery was typical of the South as a whole in 1955.

The Montgomery Bus Boycott

Any attempt to defy the legal statutes imposed by the white power structure was an offense unofficially punishable by death. Mr. E. D. Nixon, president of the Montgomery chapter of the NAACP, knew this when he called for a boycott of the Montgomery bus system in the wake of Rosa Parks's arrest.

The response from the African-American community was overwhelming. Buses rumbled through the streets of Montgomery's African-American districts empty; people refused to ride them. Encouraged, Nixon called for a meeting of the black leadership. Most of the local African-American ministers heeded his call. However, the meeting got off to a rocky start when several of the preachers, afraid of the reaction of the white community, requested anonymity. Nixon was livid. He said, "We've worn aprons all of our lives. It's time to take the aprons off. If we're going to be mens, now's the time to be mens."[1]

A new preacher in town walked in late but just in time to hear Nixon's tirade. He declared, "Brother Nixon, I'm not a coward. I don't want anyone to call me a coward."[2] That afternoon the clergy formed the Montgomery Improvement Association. They called on the new preacher to lead it. His name was Martin Luther King.

Martin Luther King

Rev. Dr. Martin Luther King Jr. was born on January 15, 1929, in Atlanta, Georgia. He grew up the son of a prominent Baptist minister. His father, Rev. Martin Luther King Sr., was the pastor of the prestigious Ebenezer Baptist Church in Atlanta.

King attended Morehouse College in Atlanta and later continued his studies at Crozer Theological Seminary in Pennsylvania. He completed his academic work at Boston University, where he met his wife, Coretta Scott. Although he received invitations to pastor in the North, he returned to the South and accepted the pastorate of the Dexter Avenue Baptist Church in Montgomery.

The leadership of the Montgomery Improvement Association planned a mass meeting at the Holt Street Baptist Church. To their surprise, thousands came to participate. The church was filled to capacity. Makeshift amplifiers had be to be set up in the parking lot to accommodate the overflow crowd. That night Dr. King said, "There comes a time when people get tired of being pushed out of the glittering sunlight of life's July and left standing amidst the piercing chill of an Alpine November. We are here because we are tired now."[3]

The audience was spellbound by Dr. King's gift of oratory. The staccato clapping of thousands of hands echoed like shotgun blasts in the night. The thunder of stomping feet threatened the foundation beneath the church's carpet. Montgomery's bus boycott was formalized that night, and an outline of the principles for nonviolent resistance was introduced.

Even as the jubilant crowd spread out into the night air, King's words seemed to hang in space: "If we are wrong—Jesus Christ of Nazareth was merely a utopian dreamer and never came down to earth! If we are wrong justice is lie . . . we are determined here in Montgomery—to work and fight until justice runs down like water, and righteousness like a mighty stream!"[4] King had found the answer to the age-old question, "Who is Jesus?" That answer drove him to dream and work for righteousness and justice till the day he died.

For 381 days, Montgomery's African-American citizens refused to ride the buses. Amidst bombings, shootings and terrorist threats they remained steadfast in their goal. Nightly mass meetings at community churches bolstered their faith. Hymns and testimonies gave them courage. And then, in early 1956, the Supreme Court of the United States ruled that segregation on the buses was unconstitutional.[5]

Martin Luther King emerged from the Montgomery struggle as the new leader for black America. He and fellow clergy went on to form the Southern Christian Leadership Conference. The organization was formed to combat racism in the South and to enfranchise the African-American population. Dr. Martin Luther King Jr. would later be awarded the Nobel Peace Prize.

The Little Rock Nine

The Brown vs. Board of Education integration ruling of 1954 had been received like bitter medicine by school boards in the South. Implementation was instituted at a snail's pace. The NAACP legal team pressed for integration in the Little Rock, Arkansas, school system, and in time a group of nine students from the all-black high school was chosen to attend the previously all-white Central High School. The media tagged them the Little Rock Nine.[6]

Resistance to the idea of school integration was intense. The town's staunch segregationists bared their knuckles for a fight. Arkansas Governor Orval Eugene Faubus, a rabid segregationist, pledged "blood will run in the streets" if the black students tried to enter Central High School.[7]

Two hundred fifty National Guardsman had to be called to expedite the integration order. Melba Patillo Beals, one of the Little Rock Nine, recounted, "I'd only been in the school a couple of hours and by this time it was apparent that the mob was overrunning the school. Policemen were throwing down their badges and the mob was getting past the wooden sawhorse because the [white] police would no longer fight their own to protect us."[8]

The situation became so volatile that President Eisenhower was called on to send federal troops to Central High School.[9] The students had to be accompanied to class by United states military escort. They traveled to school in jeeps instead of school buses.

Governor Faubus ordered Little Rock's schools closed altogether in 1958. Almost half of the students enrolled in private schools; hundreds did not attend at all. In a Gallup poll taken in late 1958, Faubus was voted one of America's most admired men.[10] But the Supreme Court ruled his closing of the schools "unconstitutional," and the Little Rock school system reopened in September 1959 on a nonsegregated basis.

The Sit-In Movement

On February 1, 1960, four black undergraduate students from North Carolina AT&T College sat down at the lunch counter of the local Woolworth store. They were permitted to buy items from the store, but company policy dictated that the lunch counter was off limits to African-American patrons. The students refused to move away from the counter when they were told that they would not be served. They just sat and waited quietly. The protest continued daily as students filled the stools at opening and stayed until closing.

Young white provincials took the occasion to pour liquids on the heads of the students. They cursed them, spit on them and burned them with lit cigarettes. Still the students refused to budge. Following the lead of India's Mahatma Gandhi, they suffered nonviolently. Finally, on July 25, 1960, at 2:00 p.m., the African-American students were served at the Woolworth lunch counter at Greensboro, North Carolina. The sit-in movement was born, and it caught on like wildfire all over the South.

The Freedom Riders

In the spring of 1942 a group of Christian pacifists gathered to form a civil rights organization. They called it the Congress of Racial Equality or simply CORE. Four of the founding members were white; two were black. They believed that America was suffering from a human problem rather than a racial problem. They set out to promote the brotherhood of humankind.

On May 4, 1961, CORE resurrected a tactic that had first been used in the late 1940s. Teams of young people were recruited for what was labeled a "freedom ride." An integrated team including both white and black young people boarded a Greyhound bus. Whites and blacks sat next to each other, an illegal practice in many Southern states. The purpose was to test laws that had been passed outlawing segregation at interstate accommodations.[11]

Mayhem broke out when the bus reached Birmingham, Alabama. Klansmen set the bus on fire. The freedom riders were forced to evacuate. They ran straight into the arms of the racists. Clouds of smoke rose above Alabama as the young students were beaten with bicycle chains and baseball bats. The assaults continued for a great while before police finally arrived. Later public safety commissioner Eugene "Bull" Connor was questioned concerning the officers' slow response. Connor explained that, since the attack had taken place on Mother's Day, all of the officers had been visiting their mothers at the time.[12]

Student Nonviolent Coordinating Committee

Eventually the freedom rides were deemed too dangerous by the members of CORE. But another organization was there to pick up the charge. The Student Nonviolent Coordinating Committee or SNCC (pronounced *snick*) was founded on April 16, 1960.[13]

Ella Baker, executive director of the Southern Christian Leadership Conference, sponsored the gathering which spawned the organization. About 120 African-American student activists from fifty-six colleges and high schools answered the call to come to Raleigh, North Carolina. SNCC was to be a student movement independent of the control of the older civil rights leadership, yet dedicated to nonviolent resistance to racism.[14]

The fledgling organization continued to organize freedom rides and experienced much the same resistance as the CORE members had. A freedom ride to Montgomery, Alabama, sparked a wave of violence. Once again the police failed to show up when the freedom riders rolled into town. John Lewis, president of SNCC, was beaten terribly. Others were attacked by a mob as they exited the bus.

Attorney General Robert Kennedy begged Martin Luther King not to meet with the freedom riders when they landed in Montgomery. Perhaps he anticipated that such a meeting could spell trouble. He was right.

A special service was held at the First Baptist Church of Montgomery, where Rev. Ralph Abernathy was the pastor. The audience lifted up the anthems of freedom with renewed passion. As dark settled down upon Montgomery, spiritual darkness began to surround the church. The sounds of cursing and shouting echoed in the night beyond the stained-glass windows. First Baptist Church had been surrounded by a racist mob. The worshipers were trapped inside.

Fire bombs whistled through the air. Rocks were thrown. Dr. King commanded the parishioners to remain inside the church. A caution against panic was issued. Sensing the urgency of the matter, King placed a call to Washington, D.C. Robert Kennedy ordered federal forces to the scene immediately. James Farmer of CORE recalls what happened next:

> The mob kicked open the door and they just poured in. And people were screaming, backed up against the wall. I don't know where they came from or how they did it, but the marshals materialized in that situation. It seemed almost fictional.[15]

The SCLC chose Birmingham as its next desegregation target. "Bull" Connor was incensed that the movement had chosen his city.

Already the city had been nicknamed "Bombingham" because of the rash of terrorist attacks against its African-American citizens. On Wednesday, April 10, a local judge handed down an injunction barring any conceivable form of public protest.

The injunction was ignored. On Good Friday, Martin Luther King walked down the stone steps of the Sixth Avenue Zion Hill Church with a grim look of determination on his face. Forty marchers followed him.

A crowd of onlookers formed a gauntlet on both sides of the street. The African-Americans shouted exclamations of freedom. When King passed by, some of the crowd members dropped to their knees. He was arrested in moments.

Criticized by Peers

Six local white clergymen publicly criticized King and deemed the movement's activities in Birmingham untimely. In the darkness of a Birmingham jail cell, King wrote them a letter. One part of the letter said,

> I have traveled the length and breadth of Alabama, Mississippi and all the other Southern states. On sweltering summer days and crisp autumn mornings I have looked at her beautiful churches with their lofty spires pointing heavenward. I have beheld the impressive outlay of massive religious education buildings. Over and over again I found myself asking: "What kind of people worship here? Who is their God? . . . Where were their voices of support when tired, bruised and weary Negro men and women decided to rise from the dark dungeons of complacency to the bright hills of creative protest?"[16]

The Children's Crusade

The situation grew even more volatile as the Birmingham movement launched the "children's crusade." It was decided that the African-American children of the city would be called upon to commit their lives to the struggle.

On April 30 one of King's lieutenants handed out leaflets telling children to leave school at noon on the following Thursday and go to the Sixteenth Street Baptist Church for a march. On the Thursday, Bull Connor waited as some one thousand children came marching out of the door of the church. His patrolmen arrested six hundred African-American children.[17]

Those who escaped chanted freedom songs and prayed. Desperate, Connor ordered his men to herd the demonstrators into the park, where billy clubs whipped through the air and trained police dogs bared their fangs. Firemen turned high-pressure water hoses on the women and children at Connor's command. People flew through the air, propelled by the powerful jet streams of water. The force from the hoses was strong enough to rip the bark off of trees. Television bought the melee to the world in glorious black and white.

Even in the face of brutality the freedom fighters would not back down. Birmingham was eventually forced to concede defeat. Its downtown businesses were suffering from the lack of African-American trade. African-American faces began to appear behind sales counters in popular stores. Black men and women were given access to establishments that had denied them entrance since they opened for business.

Not all of the opposition was ready to surrender. Angry citizens bombed the Gaston hotel where King was staying. The home of King's brother, the Reverend A. D. King, was also bombed. The worst was yet to come.

On September 15, 1964, at 10:15 a.m., four little Sunday-school children were changing into their choir robes in the basement of the Sixteenth Street Baptist Church. A bomb made of fifteen sticks of dynamite exploded without warning. The blast killed the children.

The March on Washington

In 1963 a group of African-American leaders nicknamed "the big six" gathered to sponsor a civil rights march on Washington, D.C. They were Roy Wilkins of the NAACP, A. Philip Randolph of the Brotherhood of Sleeping Car Porters, James Farmer of CORE, John Lewis of SNCC, Whitney Young of the Urban League and Martin Luther King. With a contingency from the organized labor movement and a number of Northern white clergy who joined the cause, they convened the March on Washington.

A gathering of 300,000 people filled the lawn between the Washington Monument and the Lincoln Memorial. The audience included people from a wide range of religious and ethnic groups.

Around 3:00 p.m., Randolph rose to introduce the last speaker of the afternoon. He introduced King as "the moral leader of the nation."

Dr. King began to speak from a prepared text. But after a few minutes, he was soaring with spontaneous momentum. The result was the famous "I Have a Dream" speech.

The Last Civil Rights March

On June 6, 1966, James Meredith donned a pith helmet and tightened his grip on his cane. Along with four others he embarked on what he called "the march against fear." His desire was to help black Mississippians overcome their fear of voter registration. The march started in Memphis, Tennessee, and was scheduled to end in Jackson, Mississippi.

When Meredith crossed the Mississippi state line, an unemployed hardware clerk named Aubrey James Norvel stepped out from behind some bushes and shot him with a sixteen-gauge shotgun.

The civil rights community was stunned and outraged at this murder. SNCC, CORE and SCLC banded together to continue Meredith's march. A West Indian New Yorker named Stokeley Carmichael had recently been voted in as the president of SNCC. He and others took the occasion of the march to unveil their new rallying cry. They hollered, "Black Power!"

The term injected fear into whites because of its ambiguous meaning. It also split the civil rights community as organizations such as SNCC began to renegotiate the role of whites within the freedom struggle. The black nationalist doctrines of separation and self-determination began to surface. Older civil rights leaders were still committed to the ideal of integration into mainstream society. The rift in ideologies would make this the last of the great civil rights marches.

11

· ·

The Rise, Fall & Rise of Malcolm X

*M*alcolm. His presence hovered over the civil rights movement like a raven on a tree branch glaring down at a Sunday afternoon picnic. Malcolm X was the angry, implacable voice of the black Northern inner city. He had no taste for integration. In fact, he saw the civil rights movement as folly. He publicly labeled its leaders "Uncle Toms" and "sellouts."

Malcolm related well to the disenfranchised "field negro" who "caught hell" in slavery time. He saw the established, accepted black leadership as "house negroes" who kowtowed to the white power structure—and he rarely failed to say so when given the opportunity. He was a champion of the black nationalist cause.

Reactions to Malcolm X were mixed. He was despised, feared, loathed, honored and revered. Whites and many mainstream blacks shunned him as a hatemonger and demagogue. He found his larger audience among the "little negroes," the working class and poor of the urban communities. After his death, Ossie Davis eulogized him as "our living black manhood . . . and our black shining prince."

The Life Story of a Black Icon
He had been an exploiter of women, a drug peddler, a thief and a prison

inmate. In the streets of Harlem he had once been known as "Detroit Red." By his own admission he had been a hustler who lived by his wits, snorting cocaine profusely.

But Detroit Red had not been born into such an estate. He was born Malcolm Little on May 19, 1925, in Omaha, Nebraska.[1] His father, Earl Little, was an itinerant Baptist minister. On Sundays Malcolm's father preached the fiery message of the gospel, but during the week he followed the other great passion of his life: he preached the black nationalist message of Marcus Garvey and the Universal Negro Improvement Association.

Reverend Little's support of Marcus Garvey's movement was not appreciated by local whites. They warned him to get out of town. Malcolm said, "I remember being snatched awake into a frightening confusion of pistol shots and shouting and smoke and flames. My father shouted and shot at two white men who set the fire and were running away. Our home was burning down all around us."[2] This was Malcolm X's earliest vivid recollection. He was four years old.

Reverend Little moved his family to Lansing, Michigan. Here tragedy struck again. The preacher was murdered, his body left on the railroad tracks. Many believed that white racists were to blame for his death, though the story has never been proven. The Little family suffered greatly after the incident. Mrs. Little suffered a mental collapse, and the children were parceled out to various foster homes.

Despite these hardships, Malcolm proved to be an excellent student. He was the president of his seventh-grade class. He expressed an aspiration to become a lawyer. The teacher cautioned, "Malcolm, one of life's first needs is for us to be realistic. Don't misunderstand me, now. We all like you, you know that. But you've got to be realistic about being a nigger. A lawyer—that's no realistic goal for a nigger. . . . You ought to think about something you can be."[3]

Malcolm became disenchanted and surly. Finally he dropped out of school altogether and went to live with his sister Ella in Boston, Massachusetts. It was here that the slow metamorphosis from class president to first-class hustler began to take place.

Malcolm took a job on a Yankee clipper selling sandwiches before finally landing in Harlem. He was captivated by the brassy sounds of hot jazz emanating from the nightclubs. He became a chronic marijuana smoker and eventually a cocaine-snorting, gun-toting hoodlum.

A confrontation with an established Harlem hood prompted Malcolm to leave his new Harlem home for the safer environs of Boston. There he started seeing a married white woman named Laura. In time, Laura, her sister and another friend became Malcolm's burglary crew. Eventually the four of them were caught and sentenced to jail. Malcolm drew ten years in the Charlestown State Prison. It was 1946. He was twenty-one years old and hadn't yet started shaving.[4]

Malcolm "Gets" Religion

It was in prison that Malcolm first became acquainted with the teachings of the Nation of Islam. The Nation believed that God had visited Detroit, Michigan, in 1931, in the person of Master Fard Muhammad to give black people knowledge of their great place in human history.[5]

With his work accomplished, Master Fard anointed one of his followers as "the last messenger of Allah" and then left Detroit. The Honorable Elijah Muhammad, as he would come to be known, was that anointed leader of the Nation of Islam.

Malcolm wrote to Mr. Muhammad from prison. He became enamored with the teachings of the organization. Soon he was accepted as a full-fledged member. As a member of the Nation, Malcolm subjected himself to strict rules. He ate no pork, he gave up smoking, he stopped using profanity. He became a voracious reader and a self-taught man. He starred as a member of the prison debating team. Malcolm had gone into the dark bowels of a rotting, antiquated prison and earned the nickname "satan." But by the time of his release he was a model prisoner.

In the spring of 1952 Malcolm was released from Charlestown State Prison. He went to Detroit, Michigan, to live with his brother Wilfred, who was also a member of the Nation of Islam. Malcolm became deeply involved.

Elijah Muhammad demanded great discipline from his followers. They did not indulge in drinking or dancing. They were courteous and law-abiding. Members involved in sexual indiscretions were suspended from mosque activities. NOI women wore traditional Eastern garb which covered them from head to toe. The men dressed in dark suits and became recognized throughout the community for their bow ties. A paramilitary auxiliary called the Fruit of Islam kept order within the ranks.

Malcolm Takes His X

Members of the Nation of Islam substituted X in place of their last names. The X represented the name that had been stolen from the Africans when they were made slaves. The members renounced the names given to them by their white masters during slavery. They believed that one day Allah would come back and bestow unto them their original names. When asked, Malcolm said that the X meant "Ex-Smoker. Ex-drinker. Ex-Christian. Ex-slave."

Malcolm's devotion to the Nation of Islam was formally recognized when he was honored with the mantle of a minister. Eventually he was sent back to Harlem to raise Muhammad's Temple #7. There Malcolm and his congregation practiced a form of evangelism that took them to the streets of the ghetto in search of converts. They called this technique "fishing."

Some of the converts came from unlikely places. Christian churches became prime targets for the Nation of Islam evangelists. Many African-American Christians were frustrated by the white Christian community's unwillingness to accept them as fellow human beings and were attracted by Malcolm X and the Nation of Islam.

The Muslims became one of the most successful drug and criminal reformation organizations in the community. They opened up businesses. They created the *Muhammad Speaks* newspaper. Mosques opened up all over America. Malcolm X catapulted to the position of National Minister. Indeed, the American public came to associate his face as the trademark of the Black Muslim movement.

Meanwhile, the headlines were filled with the exploits of the civil rights movement in the South. Television brought images of helpless blacks being pummelled by police clubs into Northern living rooms. Malcolm watched in horror and disgust as police dogs attacked black women and children. Malcolm became extremely critical of the Civil Rights movement. He compared the nonviolent doctrines of the Civil Rights leaders to the numbing effects that novocaine gives a dental patient. He said,

> The white man . . . wants to take advantage of you and not have to be afraid of you fighting back. To keep you from fighting back, he gets these old religious uncle toms to teach you and me, just like novocaine to suffer peacefully. Don't stop suffering, just suffer peacefully.[6]

Malcolm believed that integration was a dream which would never be realized. He stated plainly, "No, I'm not an American. I'm one of 22 million black people who are the victims of Americans. One of 22 million black people who are victims of democracy. . . . And I see America through the eyes of a victim. I don't see any American dream; I see an American nightmare."[7]

Many mainstream African-American leaders tried to write Malcolm X off as an extremist. But his popularity spread in the black inner cities of the nation, especially in Harlem. Benjamin Karim said, "I have seen Malcolm hold a crowd like that spellbound, even in the rain. Their concentration so intense, forgetting even to blink until their eyes went dry, and then looking as if they were awakening from a trance, they stood there in the rain, many of them without umbrellas, listening to Malcolm X. It seemed that nothing could dampen the fire in Malcolm's words."[8]

Split with the Nation of Islam
In 1964 Malcolm X left the Nation of Islam. There were several contributing factors. Following the assassination of President John F. Kennedy, black Muslims were ordered not to make any negative statements about the fallen leader. Malcolm disobeyed. He called the murder of the president a case of the "chickens coming home to roost."[9] He believed that the climate of hate perpetrated by the United States across the world had finally come back to claim one of its own. "Being an old farm boy, chickens coming home to roost never made me sad, it made me glad," Malcolm said.[10] After this outburst, Elijah Muhammad silenced Malcolm, his top minister, for sixty days.

Malcolm X borrowed some money from his sister Ella and traveled to Africa and the Middle East. In the land of his forefathers he was treated like a traveling dignitary. Leaders from many of the Muslim nations had followed Malcolm's struggle and defection from the Nation of Islam. They encouraged him as he embraced orthodox Islam. Malcolm was given a new name: El Hajj Malik El Shabazz.

During his travels in Africa, Malcolm sought to enlist the aid of some of the African nations in the African-Americans' struggle for freedom. Malcolm wanted the African nations to support him as he brought the United States before the United Nations. He sought to charge the United States with human rights abuses of its twenty-two million black citizens.

Many people believe that this course of action was what eventually cost Malcolm X his life. He was stalked by the Nation of Islam before he died. Louis X warned in the Nation of Islam newspaper: "Only those who wish to be led to hell, or to their doom, will follow Malcolm. The die is set, and Malcolm shall not escape." But Malcolm still believed that the plot to kill him was bigger than the Muslims.

Malcolm X had come back from his pilgrimage with a new vision. He founded two new organizations. One was a religious body called the Muslim Mosque, Incorporated. The other was called the Organization of African-American Unity or OAAU. The OAAU was a nonreligious group dedicated to uniting all people of African-American descent in the struggle for freedom and dignity in America.

Inside the Mind of a Revolutionary

Like his Garveyite father before him, Malcolm was a strong believer in black nationalism. He believed that black people should determine the political structure of their community. He believed that blacks should control the economy of largely black communities. He believed that the educational system in predominantly black neighborhoods should be governed by black parents.

On February 21, 1964, Malcolm—now using his Muslim name, El Hajj Malik El Shabazz—stood up to address a crowd of four hundred at a meeting of the Organization of Afro American Manhattan. Two black men began to argue. One yelled, "Hey, man, take your hands out of my pockets." As Malcolm called for peace, a smoke bomb was dropped—a diversionary device. At least two men stood up and emptied shotguns into Malcolm as his horrified family and followers looked on.

Four members of the Nation of Islam were later arrested. However, one man arrested for his murder said that he had never seen the other men convicted of the crime before. Who really killed Malcolm X? Speculation has continued since the day of the crime. What is certain, however, is that the fallen leader redefined the struggle for black empowerment in American. He said that without political and economic freedom blacks would never be free. His words did not fall on deaf ears.

Malcolm's teachings would become the sacred canon of the coming black power movement. He forced African-American clergy to reexamine the role of the church in the community. A generation of black thought has been strongly influenced by the man who fell in a hail of bullets at the Audubon Ballroom: Reverend Earl Little's son, Malcolm.

12

· ·

The Changing
of the Guard

*I*t was August, 1965, the day after the madness. Faint clouds of angry gray smoke wafted above the broken sidewalks of the ghetto called Watts, Los Angeles. All was quiet as the sun peeked through the clouds to trumpet the dawn of a new morning.

Gone were the echoes of stampeding feet. Silence replaced the ringing of shattering plate glass, the screaming of the sirens, the fierce blackness of the night, the marching feet of five thousand national guardsmen, the burst of shotgun fire. In the wake of the uprising sat a million dollars in property damage. The most tragic statistic was the twenty-seven dead, who would never go home to their families again.

It was said that the night before, two California highway patrolmen had pulled over a car driven by a twenty-one-year-old black man named Marquette Frye. Frye was allegedly drunk and had been driving recklessly. He told the policemen, "You're not going to take to me jail."

When an officer drew a gun on Frye he responded, "Go ahead, kill me." Another officer held off the crowd with a shotgun as the other policeman successfully subdued Frye and placed him in the back seat of a patrol car in handcuffs. What happened next would change Los Angeles forever. According to one witness, "The officer took his club and kept jamming it into [Frye's] stomach. When that happened all the people standing around got mad. And I got mad. It's just too bad the officer couldn't have driven away and then struck the man. His action was breeding violence."

It wasn't long before young blacks started throwing rocks and other projectiles at store windows and passing cars. African-American citizens and white police clashed. Molotov cocktails were hurled. Tear gas canisters were lobbed through the air. Ghetto fires burned unchecked. White people were pulled from their cars and their cars were set ablaze. Stores were ransacked and pillaged as crowds of ghetto people yelled, "Burn, baby, burn." If Dr. King's words were true, if riots were really the "language of the unheard," then a neighborhood full of angry blacks was speaking with matches.[1] Riot fever spread over 150 blocks.

The Civil Rights Movement Is Challenged

King (who would not be assassinated until years after the Watts riot) was dumbfounded by the events that flooded the television screen. Against the publicly expressed wishes of the governor of California, King went to Watts. He found himself unknown and unappreciated in Watts. While there, he gave an impassioned speech on the virtues of nonviolence before three hundred people at the Westminster Community Center. In the middle of the speech a heckler interrupted, shouting, "Get out of here, King! We don't want you."[2]

Later that evening, civil rights stalwart Bayard Rustin had a chance to talk to King about what he'd found in Watts. Rustin later said, "I'll never forget the discussion we had with King that night. He was absolutely undone, and he looked at me and said, 'You know, Bayard, I worked to get these people the right to eat hamburgers, and now I've got to do something . . . to help them to get the money to buy [them].' "[3]

African-Americans in the large cities outside of the South were not impeded by any censure of their voting privileges. The segregation that closed them behind the invisible walls of the ghetto was of a de facto nature. Often, realtors in largely white communities simply would not assist African-Americans in their quest to live outside of the ghetto.

The Civil Rights Movement Goes North

Dr. King's philosophy of nonviolence was losing ground. Young blacks espousing separation under the ominous term "black power" were gaining the ears and hearts of a large cross-section of the African-

American community. King himself was considered too out of step with the pulse of the community.

The leadership of the Southern Christian Leadership Conference (SCLC) chose Chicago as its next target. It was the nation's second-largest city. Chicago was thoroughly segregated. A coalition called Coordinating Council Community Organization (CCCO) was staging demonstrations for better schools for minorities in the city. A school-teacher named Al Raby invited the leadership of SCLC to come in and assist the group in the fight for better housing and schools.

Ralph Abernathy later lamented, "We should have known better than to believe we could come to Chicago and right its wrongs with the same tactics we had used in Montgomery, Birmingham, and Selma. We entered a different world when we came to this northern city in 1966, a world we didn't fully understand. . . . It was an embittering experience and I'm not sure that Martin ever got over it."

Yes, Chicago was a different world. King marveled as he was driven over miles and miles of seemingly endless slum terrain. Abernathy said, "I recall looking over at Martin and both of us shaking our heads. The number of people living in this squalid devastation was beyond our comprehension."[4]

There were no big-bellied sheriffs spouting tobacco juice and anti-black epitaphs. There were no "white" and "colored" rest rooms. What King and his staff found was an all too accommodating Mayor Richard Daley who constantly claimed that his staff was doing all that it could to ease the poverty of blacks in the city.

Martin Luther King Jr. and Reverend Ralph Abernathy took apart-ments in one of the worst neighborhoods in black Chicago. Abernathy said,

> The odor was unbearable. It was a little like a city dump except that along with the garbage you constantly smelled human waste. There was no escaping it. The hallways were filled with rotting food and piles of feces, and always you could see the rats patrolling—so large and bold that you wondered if they weren't going to attack you.[5]

Riots in the Chicago Ghetto

One hot July day, neighborhood children were arrested by police for opening a fire hydrant. Riot fever began to kindle. Reverend King went to police headquarters and secured the release of the young people. He then went back and called for calm and peace in the neighborhood. When he started talking about the need for nonviolence, people quickly grew impatient and disgusted. Some walked away while others threw a fusillade of raw profanity at the civil rights leader. Abernathy said, "He had encountered for the first time a crowd of blacks that he could neither reason with nor overpower with his rhetoric."[6] A riot broke out.

Before he left Chicago, King led two marches for equal housing. On July 30, 1966, five hundred demonstrators marched through Chicago's Gage Park. Their goal was to hold a vigil outside a real estate office which was a known discriminator against blacks. Angry whites showered the demonstrators with debris. Cars were overturned and set ablaze. The protestors had to turn back at the advice of the police.

The next week King led a demonstration to real estate agencies in two firmly segregated Chicago neighborhoods. Angry whites were ready again. Projectiles darkened the sky. King was knocked down by a stone that hit him in the head.

In the end Mayor Richard Daley signed a covenant promising to work harder to improve housing conditions for black Chicagoans. In return the civil rights leaders agreed to halt the marches. Many black Chicagoans were hesitant to believe that Mayor Daley would abide by the agreement. However, King declared victory and went back to Atlanta.

King took back with him a memory that haunted him. He had been shocked as young blacks booed him during a Chicago rally. It had never happened before, not even before the most hostile white audience. He later reasoned,

> For twelve years, I and others like me had held out radiating promises of progress. I had preached to them about my dream. I had urged them to have faith in America and in white society. Their hopes had soared. They were now booing because they felt that we were unable to deliver on our promises. They were booing because we had urged them to have faith in people who had too often proved to be unfaithful. They were now hostile because they were watching the dream that they had so readily accepted turn into a frustrating nightmare.[7]

Louis Lomax wrote, "Chicago was a failure, not for Martin himself, but for his Christian nonviolent attack upon complex socioeconomic problems. Chicago was final evidence that the system that controls the ghetto would not yield power to the nonviolent and the civilized. Only those who were willing to burn and loot had the power to get things done."[8]

The Rise of the New Black Consciousness

By the latter 1960s African America was beginning to assert itself culturally. Chemically processed or hot-comb-straightened hairstyles were replaced by the "afro," also known as a "bush" or a "natural." An African top garment called a "dashiki" became stylish. African-Americans greeted each other with an elaborate soul handshake. The uplifted clenched fist symbolized black power.

Playwright LeRoi Jones was crafting works like *The Dutchman.* The Last Poets, a militant poetry troupe, was chanting songs with titles like "Niggers Are Scared of Revolution." James Brown, often called Soul Brother Number One, slithered and gyrated across the stage singing his number-one hit soul anthem, "Say It Loud / I'm Black and I'm Proud."

13

....

America in Flames

One hot evening in the summer of 1967, a Newark taxi driver was arrested after a traffic skirmish with local police. Word of the arrest surged through the Central Ward. Soon the fourth precinct was surrounded. Blacks began to pelt the police station with rocks and bottles. The police dispersed the crowd. However, by evening riot fever had shaken New Jersey's largest city. Governor Richard Hughes declared a state of emergency, charging that Newark had become a "city in open rebellion."[1]

Four thousand city police, state troopers and National Guardsmen struggled to bring back law and order. Jeeps and eleven-ton armored personnel carriers toting mounted machine guns advanced through the ghetto streets. Rioters looted a gun store on Springfield Avenue. They started firing off rounds at police and firemen as they marched through the heart of the ghetto. By the end of the week twenty-five people had died, and more than a thousand were injured. Thirteen hundred had been arrested.[2]

The rebellion spread. By the next week, cities surrounding Newark went up in flames. Riots shook Elizabeth, New Brunswick, Jersey City and Englewood. George S. Hatfield was the mayor of Plainfield, New Jersey, a city of fifty thousand. Hatfield claimed that his city had experienced "planned, open insurrection."[3] A mob had stomped a policeman to death. A Plainfield official remarked, "We are living in the shadow of blackmail threats by Negroes to tear the whole city apart next time."[4]

Cities from Des Moines, Iowa, to Erie, Pennsylvania, were alive with urban violence. Attorney General Ramsey Clark said that the riots could not be predicted. "It can't be graphed," he said. "The conditions have existed over many years."[5]

By sheer coincidence, the first Black Power Conference was being staged in Newark during the uprising. The conference was a meeting of the minds for the Black Power movement. Reverend Nathan Wright, the conference chairman, said, "The Negro has lived with the slave mentality too long. It was always 'Jesus lead me and the white man will feed me.' Black power is the only basis for unity among Negroes."[6]

The Voice of Rage

Twenty-three-year-old H. Rap Brown, who had succeeded Stokeley Carmichael as the president of SNCC, was one of the leading proponents of the Black Power movement. He remarked, "Color is the first thing Black people in America become aware of. You are born into a world that has given color meaning and color becomes the single most determining factor of your existence."[7] H. Rap Brown also said, "Being black in this country is like somebody asking you to play white Russian roulette and giving you a gun with bullets in all the chambers."[8] "Rap," as he was called, urged blacks to "wage guerilla war on the honkie white man." He said, "I love violence."[9]

The voices of Stokely Carmichael and H. Rap Brown produced sheer terror in the hearts of white people. Carmichael said, "We are preparing groups of urban guerrillas for our defense in the cites. The price of these rebellions is a high price that one must pay. This fight is not going to be a simple street meeting. It is going to be a fight to the death."[10]

H. Rap Brown went to Cambridge, Maryland, and gave a speech from the roof of a car. He yelled at three hundred African-Americans in the dark. Speaking of the officer murdered by rioters in Plainfield, New Jersey, he said, "Look what the brothers did in Plainfield. They stomped a cop to death. Good. He's dead. They stomped him to death."[11]

As the crowd cheered Rap cried, "Detroit exploded, Newark exploded, Harlem exploded! . . . It is time for Cambridge to explode, baby.

... Black folks built America. If America don't come around, we're going to burn America down, brother." Later he explained, "Violence is necessary. It is as American as cherry pie."[12]

In the wake of the Detroit uprising President Lyndon Johnson called for a day of prayer. In an address to the American people on July 27, 1967, he said,

> My fellow Americans:
>
> We have endured a week such as no nation should live through: a time of violence and tragedy. . . . The only genuine, long-range solution for what has happened lies in an attack mounted at every level upon the conditions that breed despair and violence. All of us know what those conditions are: ignorance, discrimination, slums, poverty, disease, not enough jobs. We should attack these conditions—not because we are frightened by conflict, but because there's simply no other way to achieve a decent and orderly society in America.[13]

Los Angeles County district attorney Evelle J. Younger commented, "We might have successfully kept the Negro in slavery, but we cannot keep him half free. It's going to cost an enormous amount to give the Negro and other disadvantaged minorities equal opportunities across the board. . . . I say, let's do it now."[14]

Memphis

In March 1968 a union of black garbage workers asked for Dr. King's help as they waged a strike against the city of Memphis, Tennessee. King and the forces of the SCLC called for a march which would take place in the downtown area. It did not go as planned.

A *Newsweek* article reported: "Summer 1968 began last week—with spring just eight days old. . . . For the first time in a decade of nonviolent agitation, Nobel laureate King lost control of a demonstration as it swept through the streets."[15]

Rev. King was despondent over the march that had turned into a full-scale riot. Still, he was determined to prove that nonviolence could succeed. Not long afterward he returned to Memphis. Plans for a new march had been thwarted by an injunction. However, Dr. King was asked to speak at the Mason Temple Church of God in Christ. His words were prophetic:

Well, I don't know what will happen now. We've got some difficult days ahead. But it really doesn't matter with me now, because I've been to the mountain top. And I don't mind. Like anybody, I would like to live a long life. Longevity has its place. But I'm not concerned about that now: I just want to do God's will. And he's allowed me to go up to the mountain, and I've looked over, and I've seen the promised land. I may not get there with you: But I want you to know tonight that we as a people will get to the promised land.[16]

King Is Assassinated

April 4, 1968, was a sunny day. Martin Luther King was in good spirits. That day he met with some of his colleagues. From his motel he phoned Ebenezer Church in Atlanta to turn in the title of the message he planned to deliver that Sunday: "Why America May Go to Hell."[17]

King stepped out on the balcony to speak to some friends below. Suddenly there was a loud explosion that sounded like a car backfiring. King slumped to the floor of the balcony. Blood streamed from a tremendous bullet wound in his right jaw. He was dead before he arrived at the hospital.

Uprising in the Streets

The next voice that America heard belonged to Stokely Carmichael. Speaking from Washington, D.C., he urged, "Go home and get your guns. When the white man comes he is coming to kill you. I don't want any black blood in the street. Go home and get you a gun and then come back because I got me a gun."[18]

Later that day twenty-seven-year-old Carmichael said, "When white America killed Dr. King she declared war on us. . . . We have to retaliate for the deaths of our leaders. The executions of those deaths [are] going to be in the streets."[19]

When a reporter asked him if he shouldn't be afraid for his life he responded, "The hell with my life, you should fear for yours. I know I'm going to die."[20]

Washington, D.C., exploded. Arson smoke obscured the tourists' view of the capitol building. Looting and burning spread to just east of the White House. Young people yelled, "Burn, baby, burn."

America's knees began to buckle as violence shook its urban cores from coast to coast. Cities all over the United States went up in flames in the wake of King's murder. Tears and firebombs were a lethal combination. Angry, defiant blacks stood crying as billowing smoke loomed overhead. America was at war with itself.

A total of 68,887 guardsmen and troops were summoned to quell the rebellions across the nation. Insurrections were staged in 129 cities in 29 states. Thirty-nine people died in what amounted to a war on American soil. Thirty-four were African-American.

Resurrection City

Ralph Abernathy assumed the reins of the Southern Christian Leadership Conference. His first project was one that the organization had been planning long before King's demise.

The Poor People's March on Washington was originally designed to dramatize before the nation the plight of America's poor. The call was made for millions of poor people to come to Washington. A shanty town was to be raised in the shadow of the Washington Monument in West Potomac Park.

In the wake of the riots Washington was leery. Citizens were already afraid. Sporadic violence was still an unwelcome reality in Washington. Senator John L. McDellam was not confident in Ralph Abernathy's abilities to maintain control. He said, "The [Senate subcommittee] has information that in meetings of militant groups they have discussed and have made the statement that, once this march reaches Washington, Abernathy [the march leader] cannot control it and that he will be pushed aside and that the two very radical and extremist leaders whom I will not name now are to take his place and lead the demonstration."[21]

We might guess that the senator was referring to Stokely Carmichael and H. Rap Brown. However, the march did not bring the anarchy that was feared. Yet it was not the success that Martin Luther King had envisioned. About thirty-five hundred people descended on what was called Resurrection City. A heavy rainstorm turned the settlement into a swamp. Gang members came and created violence and intimidation.

At a rally from Resurrection City, Abernathy cried out the demands of the marchers: "That no child go hungry . . . that no family lack good housing . . . that no man be without a job . . . that no citizen be denied an adequate income . . . that no human being be deprived of health care . . . that every American be educated to the limit of his hope and talent . . . that no more of our people be murdered by the violence which torments America."[22]

A mass arrest ended the protest called the Poor People's Campaign. The settlers were evicted from the grounds after their demonstration permit expired. Blacks all over Washington rioted that night in protest, and again the boots of National Guardsmen could be heard stomping all over the ghettoes of Washington, D.C. The civil rights movement was approaching its end.

The Black Panther Party for the Defense

By 1967 young African-Americans were becoming increasingly impatient with the slow, grinding process of the mainline civil rights community. President Johnson commissioned a blue ribbon panel to compile a fact-finding document concerning the causes of urban rioting. It said, "Segregation and poverty have created in the ghetto a destructive environment totally unknown to most white Americans. What white Americans have never fully understood and what the Negro can not forget is that white society is deeply implicated in the ghetto. White institutions created it, white institutions maintain it, and white society condones it."[23]

A new rising crop of black leaders intended to change all that. The new leaders hailed from the San Francisco Bay area, Oakland to be exact. Called the Black Panther Party for Self-Defense, the organization was anything but nonviolent. They were not civil rights workers or social activists. They were full-blown, gun-toting revolutionaries. The Panthers' visual appearance was stunning. They wore black leather jackets, black berets and black boots. They brazenly walked the streets of Oakland with shotguns and pistols raised.

The Panthers studied communist and socialist philosophies. They were courted by the Red Chinese government. They were hailed by Cuban dictator Fidel Castro. The Panthers' minister of defense, Huey P. Newton, once told his chief of staff David Hilliard, "We're going to be the personification of Malcolm's dreams."[24]

Huey P. Newton grew up in the nurturing world of the black Baptist church. His father was a preacher. As a child Newton was a member of the Baptist Young People's Union and the Young Deacons. He also attended Sunday school. Young Newton's favorite Bible story was

David and Goliath. He said, "I liked David and Goliath because despite Goliath's strength and power, David was able to use strategy and eventually gain the victory. Even then, the story of David and Goliath seemed directed to me and my people."[25]

In 1966 Huey P. Newton met a fellow Oaklander named Bobby Seale. Together with a teenager named Bobby Hutton, they formed the Black Panther Party for Self-Defense. Newton and his associates took the name *Panthers* because a panther only attacks when backed into a corner and forced to defend itself.

One of the first endeavors that the new organization embarked upon was to patrol the police. Like other inner city police departments of that time, the Oakland police lacked racial diversity and sensitivity. Incidents of brutality were high. Justice was rarely served in these matters. The course that Newton and his friends would take to correct the situation was a dangerous one.

One night the Panthers encountered members of the Oakland Police Department. "What are you going to do with that gun?" an alarmed officer asked Newton. Newton responded, "What are you going to do with your gun? Because if you try to take this gun, I'm going to shoot you swine."[26] Newton knew his rights. He had studied the legality of carrying firearms as a law student in college.

Word of the Black Panthers spread through the black community quickly. Huey P. Newton and Panther Chairman Bobby Seale were overnight icons. In February of 1967 Betty Shabazz, Malcolm X's widow arrived in Oakland, California. Several black organizations had invited her to the Bay area to speak. She was the featured speaker at a commemoration of the death of her husband. The Black Panthers were tapped for the security detail. At some point during her itinerary, the police arrived.

The Black Panthers found themselves at a standoff with the San Francisco Police Department. Newton looked one of the officers in the eye and said, "If you start drawing there will be a bloodbath." He recalled later, "My shotgun was in ready position, safety off and shell in the chamber. The police had no shotguns, only revolvers. Had they started something, we would have wiped them out."

Eldridge Cleaver was another flagship member of the Black Panthers. Cleaver was a convicted rapist who had published a series of groundbreaking essays called *Soul On Ice*. He became the Black

Panther Party's minister of information. He played a vital role in the creation of the *Black Panther* newspaper that was sold in ghettoes and on college campuses across America.

In the March 23, 1968, edition of the *Black Panther,* Cleaver delivered this ultimatum to the police:

> Halt in the name of humanity! You shall make no more war on unarmed people. You will not kill another black person and walk the streets of the black community to gloat about it and sneer at the defenseless relatives of your victims. From now on, when you murder a black person in this babylon of babylons, you may as well give it up because we will get your [expletive] and God can't hide you.[27]

Chapters of the Black Panther Party were established all over the United States. Self-defense was the most visible aspect of the party's platform, but certainly not the most tangible. In Oakland, California, the Panthers established a free breakfast program for children. They made health-care clinics available for the community residents and provided groceries for hungry people. Young people could be seen on the corners of urban America hawking the latest edition of the Black Panther newspaper. Panthers followed police patrols, watching for brutality and explaining constitutional rights to the arrested.

The Black Panther Party will be remembered for the extreme position which they took in response to racism. On the 107th anniversary of the Emancipation Proclamation, the Black Panther Party for Self-Defense delivered this message from the steps of the capitol building in Washington, D.C.:

> The hour is late and the situation is desperate. As a nation, America is now in the middle of the greatest crises in its history. We are 25 to 30 million strong, and we are armed. We are conscious of our situation and we are determined to change it. We are not afraid. . . . For the salvation, liberation and freedom of our people we will not hesitate to either kill or die.[28]

FBI Infiltration
But trouble was on the horizon. Soon there were shootouts with the police. The FBI infiltrated Panther ranks and fueled a bloody feud

between the Black Panthers and another militant organization.

FBI infiltration and observation of black organizations was not a new phenomenon by the time the Black Panthers rose to national attention. Dr. Martin Luther King's name made Section A of the FBI's enemy list.[29] He was constantly shadowed by the Bureau's agents. His phones were tapped. Electronic listening devices were planted in his hotel rooms. The FBI convened a think tank on how to "neutralize" Dr. King.[30] A shaken King once confided in a friend, "They are out to break me."[31]

Malcolm X was also the subject of intense law enforcement scrutiny. In 1964 FBI agents followed him through Africa and the Middle East.[32] Although Malcolm drew the anger of the Nation of Islam loyalists after he defamed his former mentor Elijah Muhammad, he suspected other forces were at work to bring about his demise. Not long before his death, he said, "The more I keep thinking about . . . the things that have been happening lately, I'm not sure it's Muslims. I know what they can and can't do."[33]

The Bureau's tactics proved successful in breaking up the Black Panthers. Eldridge Cleaver had to seek asylum in Algeria. Bobby Seale was expelled from the party. Huey P. Newton faced an array of serious charges ranging from murder to embezzlement.[34]

*   *   *

African-Americans devised diverse strategies to obtain freedom and equality in America. Civil rights organizations argued for integration. Black nationalists argued for separation. Riots shook the country. Finally, civil rights legislation—even if too little and too late—began to change life in America.

Part Five

. . . .

The Post-Civil Rights Era

*B*y the 1970s much had changed America. African-Americans were hired in positions previously closed to them. Black faces appeared in high government positions. The long, hot summers of ghetto rioting had cooled in the early 1970s. Stokely Carmichael moved to Africa and changed his name. H. Rap Brown became a Muslim cleric. Members of the Black Panther Party were dead, in prison or on the run. SNCC had folded its tent. Other civil rights organizations were seeking to redefine themselves.

By the 1970s even the music had changed. The protests of the sixties were fueled by soul songs like the Impressions' "Keep On Pushing." By the mid-seventies, disco music had come of age. Young people were crowding into discotheques in platform shoes, singing along with Taste of Honey's "Boogie Oogie Oogie."

America's black middle class has grown at an astounding rate. However, the fight against racism and discrimination continues. Blacks are seeking to develop methods to fight racism, which now usually comes couched in political correctness. The opponents of affirmative action have sought to use Dr. Martin Luther King's image and snippets of his message to defend their position. Race may again be the defining question in the twenty-first century.

Contrary to popular belief, the Civil Rights movement did not die in the sixties. The movement became less visible in the media; many of its tactics became outmoded. But it continues until this day. Organizations like the Urban League, NAACP, the SCLC, the Rainbow Coalition and others still spearhead the struggle for justice in America. Churches and grassroots organizations still fight to bring about a fair and equitable distribution of resources for all people in America.

Rev. Jesse Jackson dropped out of seminary at Martin Luther King's request. King informed Jackson that he would learn much more from working with him than he would ever learn in the seminary. Jackson remains the one dominant Civil Rights figure still on the scene who has a continuing and even heightened credibility.

In this final section we will look at the struggles that still confront African America as one century ends and another begins.

14

• •

Black Money
The Rise of the New Black Middle Class

*T*he marching theme of the civil rights movement was "We Shall Overcome." At the end of the twentieth century, in many ways that song has now become a reality. New York state comptroller Carl McCall is currently the ward of a ninety-billion-dollar pension fund. Roy Roberts is the vice president of General Motors and the head of its Pontiac Division. A. Lynn Edmonds is the vice president of worldwide operations for Xerox. Glenda Goodly McNeal is the vice president of American Express at age thirty-six.

The late Ron Brown became the first black secretary of commerce of the United States. David Dinkins rose to the position of mayor of New York City. Oprah Winfrey hosts one of the most highly rated television shows ever. Whether it was the matches or the marches, the sixties activism forced open doors that African-Americans have been able to walk through in the 1990s.

Racism, the Beast That Would Not Die
In *Two Nations: Black and White, Separate, Hostile, Unequal,* Andrew Hacker writes:

> Black Americans are Americans, yet they still subsist as aliens in the only land they know. . . . Of course, there are places where

the races mingle. Yet, in most significant respects, the separation is persuasive and penetrating. As a social and human division, it surpasses even gender—in intensity and subordination.[1]

The specter of racial injustice is as dark over the American horizon at the close of the twentieth century as it was at the end of the nineteenth century. In America race still largely determines friends, life opportunities, employment, residency and even church membership.

Will racism every be destroyed? Harvard University professor Cornel West does not think so. He writes, "I believe racism is a fundamental form of human evil, and I do believe that human evil [cannot be eliminated] in the human form. I think it can be changed, reformed, ameliorated, but it will always take some form."[2]

Statistics show that black males with college degrees earn $764 for each $1,000 earned by white males. In 1970 black families' incomes were $613 for each $1,000 of white families' incomes; by 1992 that number had fallen to $544.

Black attorneys suffer from grave inequity in America. Black attorneys between 35 and 45 years old earn on average 79 cents per dollar earned by white attorneys in the same age bracket. A survey conducted in 1987 found that only two percent of the work force of the largest 250 law firms was African-American. Fewer than 1 percent of these firms had African-American partners. A 1988 survey found that less than a quarter of one percent of America's accounting firms had at least one black partner. The number came to 37 out of 20,000 partners. Not one of the 37 blacks was in a top position.[4]

The black middle class has often found its efforts to integrate predominantly white suburbs futile. They have sometimes been met with a phenomenon called "white flight." As black families begin to move into a white neighborhood in appreciable numbers, "For Sale" signs begin to appear on lawns all over the community. The exodus of whites in response to their new black neighbors, author Kofi Buenor Hajor writes, helps to create a "stark physical division between the world of black and white America."

About one-third of all blacks live in totally segregated ghettoes.[5] In 1993, 86 percent of suburban whites lived in neighborhoods that were less than 1 percent black.[6]

Blacks earning over $50,000 a year are more likely to be segregated than Hispanic-Americans earning just $12,500 a year. In one poll 73 percent of all whites interviewed said that they would be unwilling to move into a community were 36 percent of the residents were African-American.[7]

The Bell Curve

Social pundits have listed many reasons for the economic disparities between black and white America. Few of the explanations have captured more attention than the one offered in *The Bell Curve.* The authors use scientific "data" to prove that blacks are genetically inferior to whites, a condition that plays itself out on a cognitive level. They write:

> The evidence presented here should give everyone who writes and talks about ethnic inequalities reason to avoid flamboyant rhetoric about ethnic oppression. Racial and ethnic differences in this country are seen in a new light when cognitive ability is added to the picture. Awareness of these relationships is an essential first step in trying to construct an equitable America.[8]

These writers even go so far as to ask,

> If it were known that the black-white difference is genetic, would I treat individual blacks differently from the way I would treat them if the differences were environmental?[9]

The Media and Black America

Print and electronic media give entrance to the only African-Americans that some whites will see or hear during the course of a week. However, statistics show that the industry has consistently defied attempts at integration. Only 6 percent of broadcast industry management positions are held by African-Americans, and only 3.1 percent of all print media positions. Forty-five percent of all newspapers do not have any black reporters on the payroll. Media conglomerate Time-Warner had no black executives in its huge magazine publishing department until 1993.[10]

Shows like *Cops* and *America's Most Wanted* bring a steady stream of black miscreants and deviants into white households. Many African-American comedy shows cast blacks as harmless clowns of dubious intellectual capacity. Sometimes they are shown cross-dressing; often they mutilate their lines as though English were their second language.

In the 1980s and 1990s too many cinema productions have shown blacks as either oversexed or drugged out, bugged and dangerous. A string of "hood" movies star black males as unemployable, irresponsible, violent, semiliterate proponents of the thug lifestyle. If whites form opinions of African-Americans using these images as a measuring rod, race relations will continue to suffer.

Affirmative Action

The legacy of the Civil Rights Legislation was the affirmative action programs. These measures demanded that women and minorities be awarded slots on university enrollment lists and in the hiring halls of America. From their inception in the 1960s until today, the programs have been under fire.

In the 1990s the University of California at Berkeley became the center of the storm of controversy concerning affirmative action. A ballot initiative called Proposition 209 was placed before the voters. Activists predicted that life in California would return to pre-Civil Rights era standards if the measure passed. A popular bumper sticker read: THE FUTURE IS ON THE LINE—VOTE "NO" ON 209!

On August 28, 1997, Reverend Jesse Jackson led a protest march called "Save the Dream." The focus of the march was to raise public consciousness about Proposition 209. The march took place on the thirty-fourth anniversary of the March on Washington. Jackson led an estimated ten thousand marchers across the span of San Francisco's Golden Gate Bridge. At the march's conclusion he stated, "The dream is under siege in California. The violence of exclusion and elimination has rebounded with fierce determination and the resurrection of the walls that divide." Despite his efforts, Proposition 209 passed by a slim margin in the state of California.[11]

Affirmative action came under fire, but not just from whites. Black conservative republicans who had gained a new voice in the Reagan era were in the fight to abolish the measures. Clarence Thomas, an African-American appointed to the Supreme Court to replace Thurgood Marshall, stood at ground zero of the debate. He consistently voted against measures related to affirmative action. William E.

Nelson, a professor of political science and black studies at Ohio State University, said this of Clarence Thomas: "He makes Booker T. Washington seem like a member of the Black Panthers."[12]

An issue of *Emerge* magazine, a black affairs periodical, printed on its cover an artist's depiction of Judge Thomas dressed as a lawn jockey. Joseph Lowery, president of the Southern Christian Leadership Conference, likened Thomas to Judas Iscariot and urged blacks to pray for him.

In 1993 before the Equal Employment Opportunity Commission, Thomas confessed that affirmative action had changed his life. He said, "These laws and their proper application are all that stand between the first seventeen years of my life and the second seventeen."[13] Still, Thomas commented after a 1995 anti-affirmative action ruling that "affirmative action pins minorities with a badge of inferiority and may cause them to develop dependencies or to adopt an attitude that they are entitled to preferences."[14]

Shelby Steele, a leading black conservative, believes that blacks make too much of racism. The Stanford University professor states, "Year after year my two children are the sole representatives of their race in their classrooms, a fact they sometimes have difficulty remembering. We are the only black family in our suburban neighborhood, and even this claim to specialness is diminished by the fact that my wife is white."[15]

Dr. Steele informs us that "somewhere inside every black is a certain awe at the power and achievement of the white race."[16] He believes that the greatest detriment to black progress is a long memory of the oppression that they have faced in America.

Ward Connerly, a regent at the University of California—Berkeley, is one of affirmative action's leading opponents. Newt Gingrich, speaker of the House of Representatives, compares Connerly to South Africa's Nelson Mandela and Poland's Lech Welesa. He once promised Connerly "an all-out effort to end affirmative action racism in America."[17] Connerly says, "You can call me black, but I'm not African-American."[18] Speaking to African-Americans, he said, "We're not going to give you a lifetime membership in the 'victims club of America' because of what happened to your ancestors."[19] Connerly was one of the most visible supporters of Proposition 209. Connerly said, "It's time to end quotas. We need to even the playing field for all workers and make everyone equal once and for all."[20]

Ironically, Connerly's contracting company profited handsomely from minority set-asides during the 1980s and early 1990s.[21] However, he led a successful fight to have the measures abolished in California. The effects of Connerly's work were immediately apparent. Minority enrollment in the University of California system plummeted.

Economist Claud Anderson writes: "Black conservatism is as old as black enslavement. . . . Black conservatives operate under misleading colors. As an old farmer said, 'They run with the hounds while pretending friendship and brotherhood with the rabbits.' The confusion caused by their schizophrenic behavior provides a public cover for anti-black attitudes and activities and makes them appear as nothing more than racists in black-face minstrel make up."[22]

Economic Empowerment Needed

As Dr. Martin Luther King said years earlier, the black community suffers from a lack of economic empowerment. Political sectors of the community may disagree on the reasons why this is so. However, few disagree that it is indeed a problem. Talk-show host Tony Brown says, "Over the past twenty-five years, the black community has had a major thrust in politics and civil rights. We staged freedom marches, but we have never stopped to think about what really buys freedom. It isn't workout shoes, and it isn't even civil rights legislation. True freedom springs from economic parity with other Americans. Money is not everything but I rate it right up there with oxygen. After one hundred years of social engineering, blacks can sit next to white people in classrooms and restaurants and on planes—but can they afford it?"

During a 1983 commemoration of the March on Washington, Reverend Jesse Jackson said:

> Twenty years ago, we came to these hallowed grounds as a rainbow coalition to demand our freedom. Twenty years later, we have our freedom—our civil rights. . . . But twenty years later, we still do not have equality. We have moved in. Now we must move up. Twenty years ago, we were stripped of our dignity. Twenty years later, we are stripped of our share of power. The absence of segregation is not the presence of social justice or equality.[23]

15

....

African-American in the Inner City

*D*erek Peters was raised in the housing projects of a teeming urban center called Elizabeth, New Jersey.[1] Though he is a son of the inner city, Derek is not a product of the streets. He is, however, a member of a troubled age bracket among African-American males. In 1993 there were 1,985,000 black men in prison, on parole or in jail, with 32.2 percent of all African-American men under the supervision of the criminal justice system. Only 1,412,000 African-American males took the road to college.[2] Today black males represent 46 percent of the United States prison population.[3]

At twenty years old, Derek is any mother's dream. He is intelligent, respectful and responsible. He holds down two part-time jobs while attending college on a full-time basis. Derek is a member of the InterVarsity Christian Fellowship chapter at his college. As if that were not enough, he does volunteer work in two separate programs where he mentors "at-risk" inner-city boys.

Today Derek appears troubled. His lanky six-foot-two frame shifts uneasily in the wooden folding chair. His brooding, dark brown eyes become animated as he conveys the dramatic episode that occurred not twenty-four hours ago.

"I was down at Jimmy's," he begins slowly.

Jimmy's is an institution in Elizabeth. The area that surrounds the barber shop is seedy and run-down. Drugs, crime and white flight have picked the carcass of the neighborhood clean. Jimmy's Barber Shop has been fortunate enough to make a living out of the remains.

Derek recalls,

We were all sitting there waiting for our turn in the chair. People were just shooting the breeze. I was reading a magazine, and I barely looked up when they came in.

The door opened and a brother that I knew from back in high school named James walked in. James is a street hustler. He wore baggy pants and he had braids in his hair. His "boy" (buddy) walked in behind him. They greeted everybody, they walked around, shook hands, and then they left. I didn't realize that they had been scheming.

Twenty minutes later James and his friend were back. They bum-rushed the door. They were inside real quick. They walked over to one of the customers, a brother who looked to be about my age, and said, "Come on, get up, let's go."

I didn't know the guy, but obviously they did. When homeboy hesitated, they just started swinging on him. He tried to ball himself up to ward off the blows.

When they reached for their pistols, everyone scattered for cover. They were planning to pistol-whip that kid right there in the barber shop! Right then Jimmy and the other barber came over to break it up. As James and his boy were leaving they yelled at the brother, "Don't come back to Elizabeth!" When it was all over the brother just sat there. Jimmy and everyone else told him it was time to "get out of Dodge." They tried to insist that he leave before they came back for a third visit. The brother made a phone call and this girl came to pick him up.

To everyone's surprise, the victim returned approximately a half an hour later. According to Derek, this time he had a strange bulge protruding beneath the waist band of his jacket. He had armed himself.

Fortunately James and his friend did not return. Derek informs us that if they had, there would have undoubtedly have been a shootout.

"Man," Derek continues, "these brothers are dealing with so much frustration and rage. They are burning up with anger and self-hate.

Most of the brothers in the hood don't have a purpose in life or a vision. The world around them doesn't exist. All they care about is the hood."

Derek surmises that James's troubles with the young man might have stemmed from an incident at a party or a dispute over drug turf. "They might have killed that brother, and probably over nothing," he concludes.

Mean Streets

Children's activist Marian Wright Edelman laments, "Every forty-five seconds a black child drops out of school. Every fifty seconds a black child is arrested. Every two minutes a black baby is born into poverty. Every six minutes a black baby is born at a low birth weight. Every four hours a black child is killed by gunfire."

The poison of the streets can set in early, as attested to by the life of young Robert "Yummy" Sandifer. Yummy's mother was a teenage drug addict who had been arrested forty-one times, mostly for prostitution. Before he was twelve years old, Sandifer became a member of Chicago's notorious Black Disciples street gang.[4]

Yummy became a car thief, an arsonist and a strong-arm extortionist. He ended up shooting a fourteen-year-old girl to death with a 9-mm hand gun while aiming at rival street gang members. Yummy was gunned down not long later. He was thirteen years old. His family placed a copy of his mug shot on the casket. It was the only picture of him they could find.

One of Yummy's neighbors commented, "If you make it to nineteen years old around here, you are a senior citizen. If you live past that you're doing real good."

Ghettoes like the one which murdered Yummy exist in both small and large cities across the nation. The violence is increasing at an incredible rate. In 1989 homicide was the leading cause of death for black males between the ages of 15 and 24.[5] That same year, while the average American had a 1 in 333 chance of ever being murdered, African-American males had a 1 in 21 chance of being murdered before their twenty-first birthday.[6]

The school system has failed young inner-city kids. Almost fifty years after the Brown vs. Board of Education ruling, America's inner-city schools are separate and unequal. Not only are the ghetto schools segregated, they are inadequately funded.

According to a *New York Times* article, "In 1990, predominantly white schools with low poverty levels spent an average of $6,565 per student, while those with higher poverty levels and more minorities spent an average of $5,173 per student." While 86 percent of science teachers in white schools are certified in their field, only 54 percent of science teachers in largely minority schools are certified. Close to one in four schools in urban areas reported that they could not fill an opening with a qualified teacher in 1991.[7]

Jobless in America

Sociologist William Julius Wilson points out that many of the major manufacturing jobs that employed black men in past years have fled the inner cities. Some of them have gone overseas as our country becomes part of the global economy. According to Wilson, "In the twenty-year period from 1967 to 1987, Philadelphia lost 64 percent of its manufacturing jobs; Chicago lost 60 percent; New York City, 58 percent; Detroit, 51 percent."[8]

Young men who would have been gainfully employed years back now find the job market discouraging. Many of the old jobs are obsolete; many of the new ones require specialized training. Low-skilled jobs that paid a living wage have often been moved from the cities to the suburbs.

Rev. Craig E. Sories, a minister in Atlanta, Georgia, heads Victory House, a ministry to African-American and Latino men. He says, "We are living in the information age, and the average black American has been totally left out of the technological transformation. They are living in a Third World culture in the richest and most advanced country in the world."[9]

Often poor ghetto dwellers cannot afford cars that would enable them to go out to the suburbs where there are more job opportunities. The rate of joblessness has turned these communities into pools of negativity.

In America wealth and income determine an individual's standing in the community. Psychologists William H. Grier and Price M. Cobbs examine this in *Black Rage*. "As boys approach adulthood, masculinity becomes more and more bound up with money making. In a capitalist society, economic wealth is inextricably interwoven with manhood. Closely allied is power—power to control and direct other men, power to influence the course of one's own and other lives."[10]

The Drug Trade
Each year billions of dollars' worth of illicit narcotics flow through the streets of the ghetto. The industry flourishes amidst pain and poverty, but the huge profits derived from it are banked by forces outside of the community. A popular urban folk saying is, "Black people don't own no poppy fields."

Some African-American males have sought to find a measure of wealth in the street-level drug trade. In the early 1970s Gordon Parks Jr. directed a movie called *Superfly*. Superfly was the tale of a Harlem cocaine dealer named Priest. Priest wore high-fashion clothes. He drove a beautiful custom-made Cadillac. He had two beautiful girl-friends. Priest had no illusions of ever being accepted into the main-stream of American life. He was an outlaw who would rather face death and imprisonment at any given moment than live within the means that his legitimate job skills might allow him.

Superfly was Hollywood's first true look at the drug trade in America's ghetto. However, more than twenty years after the release of the movie, the ghetto's underground economy would skyrocket. It would all be due to the creation of a new product. In the mid-1980s a potent cocaine derivative called crack first appeared on the streets of America's ghettoes.

Rock Cocaine
If a capsule of crack could be sold with a surgeon general's warning, the label might read: "One hit is not enough and a thousand is never too many." The short but expensive euphoria that crack addicts experience has created a tremendous boost to the ghetto's underground economy.

The crack trade is violent. Members of drug gangs or individual entrepreneurs go to war over lucrative inner-city blocks of territory. Kidnappings and murder are both occupational hazards.

Lorenzo "Fat Cat" Nichols ran the Jamaica, Queens, section of New York City in the late 1980s. That is to say, he controlled the crack traffic in that lower-middle-class African-American enclave. From his store-front on 150th Street, the New York legend ruled a posse of ruthless thugs who gutted the community with bottled poison. A generation of the best and brightest minds in Jamaica, New York, were sapped of their creativity by the potent drug. Eventually, Fat Cat and his crew were arrested and convicted for the murder of a twenty-four-year-old police officer named Edward Byrne. He was shot to death as he dozed in his patrol car—apparently killed to send a message to the police department.[11]

Fatherless in the Ghetto

Almost 70 percent of all young African-American children are born outside of wedlock.[12] With no father at home, the child looks to figures outside of the home to define what manhood should be. Carol Adams, director of the Chicago Housing Authority's resident programs, said (speaking of the Gangster Disciples and Vice Lords street gangs), "They are the premier social and economic organizations of the community."[13] Speaking of the gangs, Chicago policeman Donnie Hixion said, "They are sometimes literally father, brother, uncle, or their substitutes, and often the only acceptable male role models there are."[14]

Gangsta Rap

Hip hop music is the sound track of young urban America. Some hip hop extols the virtues of young love and the glory of fast cars. Some songs encourage young black men to stay in school or to be responsible for their children.

However, gangsta rap stands at the creative cutting edge of the art form. Both its audiences and its artists place a high premium on "keeping it real." The ghetto is exalted as the scenario of adventure and daring. Violence is often justified. Black-on-black crime is glorified. Women are denigrated as whores and female dogs. Skits that simulate the murder of one black by another are not uncommon.

Some hip-hop artists have names like Mobb Deep, Ghostface Killa, Ol' Dirty Bastard, Capone, Noriega, Trigga the Gambler, and Smooth the Hustler. Titles like "Pimpin' Ain't Easy," "How I Could Just Kill a Man" and "The Nigga Ya Love to Hate" have been favorites. In the past, CD covers have displayed colorful photographs of popular rappers carrying high-power firearms and strapped into bulletproof vests.

Beer and marijuana are revered as holy sacraments. Hip-hop stars rap about their love of the "chronic" or the "bud." They pose with thick marijuana cigarettes called "blunts" on their album covers and in magazines. Rappers like Snoop Doggy Dog and Ice Cube have appeared as advertising front men for St. Ides, an extra-high-potency ale sold largely in America's ghettoes.

In a magazine interview, Ice Cube said, "Nobody told me about the struggle, so I didn't know how to continue the struggle. I just know that you have to get yours and don't worry about nobody."[15]

Tupac Shakur was also one of gangsta rap's premier stars. He was the son of former Black Panther Afeni Shakur. Tupac Shakur's poignant poetry was thoroughly laced with profanity. He found himself at the center of a controversy involving factions of the East and West Coast rap worlds.

On September 7, 1997, Tupac Shakur and members of his traveling party were involved in an altercation in a Las Vegas casino. A young man was stomped and beaten in the fray. Moments later a late-model white Cadillac pulled up beside a BMW driven by Shug Knight, owner of Death Row Records, who had Shakur with him. Windows broke as bullets invaded Knight's BMW. Shakur was shot several times. A few days later he died in a Las Vegas hospital.[16]

The object of much of Shakur's constant fury was a six-foot-three, over three-hundred-pound rapper named Notorious B.I.G., a.k.a. Biggie Smalls. Biggie (given name Christopher Wallace) was twenty-four years old. On March 8, 1997, the world seemed to be in the palm of his hand. That night he would appear on the South Train Music Awards. In a few days his second album would be released.

The name of the album was *Life After Death . . . Do Us Part*. Advertisements for the album showed the dapper rap star standing in a graveyard leaning on a tombstone. Emblazoned across his chest was the Scripture verse "Whosoever believeth in him should not perish but have eternal life."

That night as Notorious B.I.G. left a party, a dark green car pulled beside his Suburban. An unseen hand pulled out a 9-mm pistol and began to fire into his body. He was rushed to a nearby hospital but was pronounced dead a few minutes after arrival.

New Orleans rapper Master P commented, "We've gotta make some changes. We created our own monster. This is supposed to be the rap game, but we call it the new wave dope game because it gets so deep. We're killin' our own mouthpieces."

In the wake of the hip-hop killings, a call came from Chicago, summoning the leading names in rap to a summit—a meeting with the man considered by many young blacks the most respected clergy-man in America.[17] Certainly he was the only one who would have received such a response to an invitation of this sort. Snippets of his recorded sermons appear in some of their songs. Public Enemy once declared him a "prophet" in their epic 1998 recording "Bring the Noise."

The month after Notorious B.I.G.'s slaying, Ice Cube chartered a private jet to take him to Chicago. Many of the other leading names in the rap industry met him there, including multiplatinum selling rapper Snoop Doggy Dog. The purpose of the trip? Some of the largest names in hip hop came to meet with Minister Louis Farrakhan of the Nation of Islam.

16

. . . .

The Second
Resurrection
The Rise of the Nation of Islam

For as lightning that comes from the east is visible even in the west,
so will be the coming of the Son of Man" (Mt 24:27). These words are
written about the return of Jesus. But W. D. Fard's followers claim that
Fard is the fulfillment of that biblical prophecy. He is a mysterious figure
in the annals of African-American history, a shadow across the page. His
name is still a word whispered in reverence among his followers.

He set foot on the shores of North America in the summer of 1930.
Three and a half years later he vanished completely. W. D. Fard's
visual image is captured in a slightly out-of-focus photograph. The
grainy black-and-white portrait offers a glimpse of a well-dressed
young man of slight build. He bows slightly while peering into what
appears to be a book of Scripture. His lips are thin; his hair is straight.
Apart from his swarthy complexion, he does not appear to exhibit any
negroid features at all.

Fard could be seen walking through the ghetto streets of Detroit,
Michigan, at the height of the depression. Beneath his arm he carried
door-to-door salesman's wares. He dazzled poor blacks with beautiful silk
scarves and thrilled them with stories of their African past. He told them
they were descendants of kings and queens in Africa. Fard told his
followers that God himself was black. Interest in his message grew so
rapidly that he and his followers had to rent a building to house them all.

Elijah

In the summer of 1931 Nation of Islam Temple Number 1 had a visitor. Elijah Poole was a young African-American, short of stature, with delicate features and a caramel complexion. The son of a Baptist preacher, young Elijah had migrated north from Sandersville, Georgia, in hope of a more prosperous life. What he found in Detroit was joblessness and the abject poverty of slum living. He soon found himself battling the demons of depression and alcoholism.

Not long after he met Fard, Poole approached him with a burning question. He later recalled, "I asked him was he our long awaited Jesus that the world been looking for the past two thousand years? Fard said, 'Yes I am the one that the world has been looking for the past two thousand years.' "

Poole was given the name Elijah Muhammad upon conversion to Islam. When W. D. Fard left Detroit, never to be seen again, Muhammad rose to the position of "the last messenger of Allah." Elijah Muhammad claimed that Islam had existed before Adam. He said, "It existed sixty-six trillion years ago when the earth and the moon were together and formed one and the same planet."[1] He taught that a black scientist named Yacub was rebuffed in his efforts to persuade the citizens of the original planet to change their native tongue. In his anger he drilled a shaft that went five thousand miles deep into the planet. He filled the giant hole with explosives and then detonated it. The explosion separated the moon from the original planet and sent it hurtling twelve thousand miles into space. The moon dropped all of its water on the earth during the great cataclysm. Muhammad explained, "That is why three-fourths of the earth's surface is covered by water and also why there is no life on the moon."[2]

Elijah Muhammad also declared, "The Original Man, Allah has declared, is none other than the black man. He is the first and the last, and maker and owner of the universe; from him came all—brown, yellow, red and white."[3]

The Muslims taught that white humanity was grafted by the wicked Yacub, 6,645 years ago. Elijah Muhammad called Yacub's creation "the serpent, the dragon, the devil and Satan."[4]

Elijah Muhammad believed that "Christianity is a religion organized and backed by devils for the purpose of making slaves of black mankind." He called the Bible "the graveyard of my poor people." The patriarch of the Nation of Islam believed that black preachers were white society's most effective tool in keeping the black population pacified and in check. According to Muhammad, the preacher "urges [black people] to fight on a foreign battlefield to save the white man from his enemies; but once home again, they must no longer be men. Instead they must patiently present themselves to be murdered by those they saved."[5]

The Conversion of Minister Farrakhan

In February 1955 a well-known calypso singer from Boston, Massachusetts, crowded into a Nation of Islam rally in Chicago, Illinois. Louis Walcott had been reared in the Christian faith. He had served as an altar boy at St. Cyprian's Episcopal Church in Boston.

In later years he recalled the circumstances that surrounded his conversion to Elijah Muhammad's fold. He said, "I hated the fact that as Christians we talked about the 'love of Christ,' but I didn't feel the love of white Christians toward black Christians. And that the church was unwilling or unable to address specific concerns of black people for justice. I went looking not for a new religion but for new leadership that would address the concerns of black people."[6]

Upon his conversion to Islam, Louis Walcott (now Louis X) used his considerable musical abilities to record a song which became the Nation of Islam anthem in the 1960s: "A White Man's Heaven Is a Black Man's Hell." This handsome, articulate convert quickly rose up in the Muslim ranks. Elijah Muhammad eventually changed his name from Louis X to Minister Louis Farrakhan.

The man known as the Honorable Elijah Muhammad died in 1975. His son Wallace Deen Muhammad ascended to the leadership of the Nation of Islam. His brother, Nathan Muhammad, said, "I know that before Wallace was born, Master Fard, to whom all praise is due, wrote his name in our home on the wall in capital letters. Wallace used to trace the letters over and over with his fingers."[7]

Under New Management

Wallace Muhammad was a scholar of Islam, a Muslim purist. He instituted sweeping reforms within the Nation of Islam. He ordered the Fruit of Islam disbanded, calling it a "punch your teeth out" outfit.[8]

Wallace inherited a thriving enterprise of seventy-six temples, thirteen thousand acres of farmland, a fish import business, restaurants, bakeries and supermarkets.[9] Under his leadership the Nation's considerable business assets were sold off. Mosques were given autonomy from the Chicago hierarchy, which had discouraged corruption. The new leader encouraged his followers to adopt true Muslim names instead of X's.

Wallace Muhammad dismissed the Yacub theology. He went as far as to refute the deity of W. D. Fard, stating, "The man came with reverse psychology and he began convincing people of the black community in America that he was a saint or a mystic or perhaps even God in the flesh. I am convinced that he himself never told anyone that he was God in the flesh, but I strongly believe that he hinted it intentionally so that others would say that he was God in flesh."[10] Wallace said that his father had been "sincere" but "misinformed" through a lack of education.[11]

Then came the last straw. Wallace D. Muhammad declared that Islam was a religion that was free of color restrictions. He removed barriers which previously barred white people from joining the Nation of Islam.

On October 18, 1976, the Nation of Islam was disbanded. Wallace Muhammad founded his own organization called the World Community of Al Islam in the West. He said, "We're a . . . community that encompasses everybody. We have Caucasians and Orientals who are members and we are all just Muslims."[12]

There was a massive falling away. Farrakhan was one of those who left. Before he made his exit he faced Wallace and said, "You got a nerve not wanting to speak [your father's] name, and he built this house. He gave you everything you have."[13]

A few months later Louis Farrakhan was back in "the wilderness of North America" preaching the original tenets of the Nation of Islam. Farrakhan barnstormed the country, gathering the faithful together around his leadership. In 1981 six thousand people attended the Savior's Day Convention held yearly to commemorate the birthday of the Honorable Elijah Muhammad.

The Nation of Islam purchased the beautiful Mosque Myriam from Wallace's bankrupt organization for 3.2 million dollars. They were also able to purchase Elijah Muhammad's Chicago mansion, where Farrakhan's family and several chief aides came to reside.

Reaching Out

In 1984 Minister Farrakhan received a call from the Reverend Jesse Jackson. He was enlisted to help negotiate the release of captured African-American military serviceman in Syria. Farrakhan impressed the Syrian diplomats by calling each meeting to order with the recitation of an Arabic prayer.[14] When Jackson ran for president in 1984, Farrakhan became alarmed by death threats from the Jewish Defense League against the candidate's life. Soon Jackson was surrounded by a cadre of battle-ready Fruit of Islam members sworn to protect his life. At the 1984 Savior's Day celebration Farrakhan warned, "If you harm this brother, I warn you in the name of Allah, this will be the last one you harm."[15]

Power, Products and Protection

In keeping with Elijah Muhammad's "do for self" philosophy, the Muslims came upon the idea of establishing a line of grooming products called Power. They established the venture with a five-million-dollar interest-free loan from Libya's President Muammar al-Khadafy.[16] Khadafy was on the United States's enemy list and even became the subject of a bombing raid and subsequent embargo. Government officials were outraged at the Nation's ties to Khadafy. Fearful, magazines refused advertising for Power products.

The Nation of Islam's security forces were hired to patrol crack- and violence-ridden housing projects in major cities. The Muslims, though skilled in martial arts self-defense tactics, did not carry weapons. However, there were stunning results. One Washington, D.C., merchant said, "There used to be shootings all the time. . . . Drug dealers used to surround my truck. The Muslims keep them away."[17]

In 1995 Minister Louis Farrakhan crisscrossed the nation speaking to rallies for black men only. Thousands of black men filled stadiums and sporting arenas across America to hear the Nation of Islam leader. Farrakhan called upon black men to be responsible fathers and leaders within their communities. He was also there to present a call. He challenged one million black men to join him in Washington, D.C., on October 16 for a "day of atonement."

The posters that beckoned black men to Washington from all across the country contained the singular image of Minister Louis Farrakhan, superimposed over a crowd of black men. However, many black men had difficulty with some of Minister Farrakhan's past statements about whites and Jewish people, and Farrakhan faced ridicule as many said that the numbers would not come to the event. As October 16 came closer on the calendar, the talk in black barber shops, Masonic halls and even churches was about the Million Man March. On the morning of October 16, black men began to pour into the nation's capital. They came from all over the United States in response to the call.

On that cool, sunny autumn day the attention of the world was focused on the mall in Washington, D.C. Stevie Wonder sang, Maya Angelou read poetry, Jesse Jackson orated. Thousands and thousands of black men came together. Fathers came along with their sons. Strangers embraced. Men cried. As the day ended, Farrakhan led the participants in a pledge to stop the violence that was destroying the black community and to assume responsibility for their actions.

Before the march, media personnel, politicians, even black leaders had tried to dismiss Farrakhan as a fluke, an extremist with limited appeal to African-Americans. After the march they wondered out loud if any other black leader could have called that many men to Washington.

Farrakhan was no longer a man who could be labeled and ignored. *Time* named him among the twenty-five most influential Americans in 1996.[18]

Citizen of the World

On the heels of the Million Man March, Farrakhan embarked on what was labeled the World Friendship Tour. There were meetings with President Gerry Rawlings of Ghana. Libya's Muammar al-Khadafy welcomed the Muslim leader and his party. South Africa's president Nelson Mandela met him with outstretched arms exclaiming, "Louis!" Farrakhan presented a bow tie to Mandela as a symbolic gesture. The trip went on to Senegal, Liberia, Nigeria and the Sudan.[19]

Other World Friendship Tours followed. Farrakhan maintained a very public friendship with Colonel Khadafy. In 1996 Khadafy pledged a billion dollars to help Farrakhan uplift the economically depressed blacks of America.

Government officials were incensed at what they considered collusion with the enemy. African-American leaders were also outraged as Farrakhan shook hands with African heads of state who were considered despots with massive civil rights violations. He even went to the

Sudan, where it is documented that slavery exists till this very day.

However, Minister Farrakhan's grassroots credibility remained intact. Jason Broom, a twenty-six-year-old who works with gangs in Kansas City, Missouri, says, "I love Farrakhan without question or reservation. I don't practice his religion but I support him. He never turned on us on the street. He's for turning us into men."[20]

On the first anniversary of the Million Man March, a reported 230,000 joined him in front of the United Nations building in New York as he asked, "Can the United Nations avert the War of Armageddon?"[21]

Farrakhan's Christian Following

Farrakhan has found a listening ear in the black Christian community. He is often a featured speaker at African-American churches. Reverend Benjamin Chavis, a prominent United Church of Christ minister and author of a Christian book of modern-day psalms, was one of the driving forces behind the scenes of the Million Man March.

Chavis, who left the NAACP presidency amid charges of adultery and financial indiscretion, later converted from Christianity to Islam to become Benjamin Muhammad. He is not alone in his support of Minister Farrakhan. Some of Minister Farrakhan's largest supporters are the Christian clergy whom he has publicly embraced in recent years.

Minister Farrakhan told Robert F. Kennedy Jr., "I have had over 2,000 Christian pastors sitting at this table over the last three or four years. As God is my witness, when we left, there was embrace. There were even tears. Even Christians who looked at themselves as prophets came and kissed my hand and pulled at my coat, saying, 'If we could just touch the hem of his garment.' "[22]

Farrakhan has toned down his early virulent antiwhite sentiments as he has mounted the international stage. Still, many wonder if he still holds to the doctrines propagated by Elijah Muhammad. The answer may be on his finger.

In place of a wedding band Minister Louis Farrakhan wears a gold ring encrusted with forty diamonds. The stones form Elijah Muhammad's silhouette. The present leader of the Nation of Islam says, "I am wedded to this man whom I believe is the Messiah." He refers to a diamond placed at the heart of the figure. He says, "I think that little, little bitty diamond represents Farrakhan."[23]

17

· ·

The Rise of the New Black Church

*E*ast Oakland, California, is a tough place to live. Beneath the towering palm trees sit humble brick-and-mortar houses with barred windows and doors. Many residents say that they feel like prisoners in their own homes. Gang activity and open-air drug trafficking hold them hostage. Prosperity has fled from the neighborhood, taking all who could afford to move along with it. Hope is a seldom-seen commodity. And yet it twinkles in the eyes of one man.[1]

The Reverend Dr. J. Alfred Smith is a spry, middle-aged man. He seems to bounce with the enthusiasm of a child on Christmas morning as he paces briskly through the gritty streets. He is unusually humble for a man of his station. Rev. Smith is one of the most prominent elders of the northern California Christian community. He pastors one of the largest African-American congregations in California. As one of the city's most powerful men, he is courted by political figures and people of national influence. But he is never beyond the reach of the people of East Oakland.

Car horns bleat greetings as he is recognized during his jaunt to another church building. He waves back as though the car contained immediate family members. Rev. Smith seems to notice everyone. A kind word is usually offered, the reward for which is a smile. He momentarily stops his scramble to corner a much taller fellow in his early twenties. He asks with a genuineness that is rare in these times, "How is your family, son?" After a brief chat, he moves down the street and on to the next person.

Smith is the pastor of the Allen Temple Baptist Church at 8500 A Street. In 1969 he assumed the pastorate of an upscale African-American Baptist church in a changing neighborhood. "There were many here who were only interested in preserving the status quo. They weren't interested in going out to make a difference in the community."

Rev. Smith would change all of that. Soon after he arrived at Allen Temple, the Black Panther Party approached him about using the church's facilities to host a free breakfast program for neighborhood children. Dr. Smith said, "Sure, we'll do anything to help as long as we don't have to carry any guns." The church's fellowship hall was also used by families waiting to be shuttled to nearby prisons to visit loved ones. The church deacons held debates with the Panthers there in the fellowship hall, over the issue of nonviolence.

As the years unfolded, several of the ex-Panthers joined Allen Temple Baptist Church. Some accepted Christ and became pillars of the church community. Eventually even Huey P. Newton's name would be added to the membership role. Following Newton's demise, Rev. Smith preached his funeral service in the sanctuary of the church. Today several thousand members fill a new facility. Allen Temple Baptist Church's list of ministries literally fills a book. Hundreds have surrendered their lives to Jesus Christ as a result of the ministry of one quiet, unassuming preacher.

Rev. Smith has no easy formula for success. He simply says: "We are to be Jesus Christ to the community. And when I look at what Jesus was, He was opening the eyes of the blind. He was helping the lame to walk. He was there preaching good news to the poor. He was there holding babies in His arms blessing them. He was there telling women that they had a sense of dignity and a sense of purpose in a society that dehumanized women. He was there saying to Peter drop your nets and follow me. He was there saying to the thief on the cross today you'll be with me in paradise. Jesus said, 'As my Father has sent me, even so I send you.' "

Allen Temple shares more than the Bread of Life with its surrounding communities. Through ministries like the Brown Bag Program, Share, Commodities and the Allen Temple Food Warehouse, the church dispenses groceries to families in need of a nutritious meal.

The beautiful brown-brick Allen Temple Arms, a senior citizens' facility, towers above the bustling streets of East Oakland. In 1995 the church received a HUD grant that is enabling it to build the first HIV/AIDS housing facility ever to be owned by a black church. Junior-high students use the church's computer lab to learn new skills on weekday afternoons. The church's credit union has made many East Oaklanders' dreams of home ownership come true. Allen also has a drug and alcohol rehabilitation center, an anger management clinic, a crisis counseling center and a job placement center.

Many find Smith's methods unorthodox. When he addresses issues like affirmative action or public school reform, members of his congregation are sometimes surprised. They wonder why a minister of the gospel would trouble himself with affairs that belong to the social or political arena.

To these naysayers he replies, "Did not Moses confront the most powerful political entity of his time, Pharaoh, and demand justice and liberation for his people? Did not Amos speak against the sins of a nation which treated the poor unfairly? As the prophet of the church, I feel that this is my responsibility."

More Urban Miracles

Rev. Smith and his congregation do not stand alone. Today, many more African-American churches are transforming whole communities and replacing despair with hope.

In southwest Houston, Texas, a ten-thousand-member United Methodist Church has a twenty-four-hour shelter for troubled youth, a housing facility for low-income families and a health clinic. A business complex called the Power Center is expected to create 221 jobs and infuse $28\frac{1}{2}$ million dollars into the local community over three years.

Rev. Floyd Flake is one of America's most prominent pastors. He serves as pastor of Allen A.M.E. Church of Southeast Queens, New York City. He further serves the surrounding community as a United States Congressman. Not only has Allen Church brought spiritual rebirth to thousands, it has also offered economic revitalization to its parish community. Allen owns a commercial strip that leases to twenty-five tenants. It owns a bus charter company and a home-care agency for senior citizens.

Second Baptist Church Cathedral in Perth Amboy, New Jersey, is another example of the transforming power of the gospel in the midst of urban America. The building itself was a condemned playhouse slated for demolition before the church purchased it in 1991. It has since been converted into an architectural marvel, complete with lavender carpeting and matching seats. Every Sunday close to two thousand worshipers crowd the facility to hear the Bible expounded by Bishop Donald Hilliard Jr. and his capable pastoral staff. Stalwarts of northern New Jersey's black middle class drive in, some from great distances, to share in the church's ministries. There are testimonies of those delivered from crime to Christ. First-time home owners, new business entrepreneurs and people returning to college as adults all point to the church's ministry in their lives.

The church owns a restaurant, a Christian academy, a family life center, a counseling center and other real estate holdings. It has been able to provide full-time employment for a number of its members. However, Bishop Hilliard's dynamic oratory centers largely around the topics of soul salvation and adherence to biblical principles as the foundation of the ministry.

Overshadowing the dais of the cathedral is an ornate stained glass window. It pictures a black Jesus Christ clad in Ghanaian ceremonial kinte cloth. Bishop Hilliard teaches that a person's pride in his ethnicity need not subtract from his piety toward God and man.

Overwhelming Growth

As baby boomers return to the sanctuaries, one trend remains consistent. Churches that were once filled predominantly by women are now attracting large numbers of male worshipers. In few places is this more evident than in the Christian Life Centre in Brooklyn, New York City. About 52 percent of its over seven thousand members are males. The Sunday turnout for services is so large that the church must turn away close to two thousand people every week.

The Reverend Dr. A. R. Bernard founded the church in 1978 after he left his job as an operations specialist at a New York banking institution. His church's literature says, "The gospel is not only salvatory but social, and, when properly communicated, can raise the quality and level of life in a community." The truth of this statement echoes through the streets of many other communities as well.

The Reverend Tony Evans, a prominent African-American evangelist and the senior pastor of Oak Cliff Bible Fellowship, in Dallas, Texas, embraces the idea of a social gospel as well. In addition to his church's impressive list of biblical training programs, the church hosts a men's fellowship called MPACT (Mentoring People According to Christ's Teaching). The goal of the program is to assist men in rising to the challenge of leadership in their churches and communities. Fatherless boys also find guidance through this ministry. In addition, Oak Cliff Bible Fellowship offers financial counseling classes as well as literacy and employment-training programs.

Looking to the Future

Back in East Oakland, Rev. Smith is realistic about the challenges facing the African-American community. He recalls, "When I was young, everybody went to church. But today it is not so. Not long ago, a little boy came up to me and said, 'Mister, I always see you going in that building [referring to the church]. What do you all do in there?' The little boy had never been inside of a church."

He also points out, "A lot of damage was done when Islamic groups began to teach young people that Christianity was a white folks' religion. It is important that our young people understand the place of African people in the biblical epic."

Dr. Smith looks at the challenges that confront the African-American community as opportunities. He is indeed optimistic. He says:

Let us, the new Sudanese, raise our hands to God. If we would climb mountains, cross deserts, conquer enemies, we must not forget to raise our hands in prayer to God. If we would form character in our children, reform our deformed institutions, inform the uninformed in society, perform as partners participating in kingdom building, be transformed by the power of the Holy Spirit, we must raise our hands in prayer to God. God will not forget us: Even in our grave God will not leave us in the dust. God will resurrect us and our works into the eternal dimensions of history, even as God raised Jesus from the dead.[2]

Epilogue

··

Deliverance

In my imagination evening was beginning to swallow the city. Soon and without warning, Harlem was enveloped in darkness. Street lamps glared, marking the way to West 110th Street and beyond. A group of young men in their late teens rushed toward us like soldiers on a military maneuver. They closed ranks, raking us over with hard stares, looking for visible wealth or weakness. I had seen them before, though they had different faces the last time. They were poor, hungry and angry. They were Harlem's young, determined to strangle a promise of survival from the night.

Grandpa kept talking as though he didn't see the youths. We had been in front of his stoop for hours. And it was night. I was fascinated by all that he knew, all that he remembered. As he finally finished his chronicle, I felt a question burning within my throat. I asked, "Now what? What next, Grandpa?"

In my imagination he pointed across the street at a building. Black iron bars guarded the beauty of its stained-glass windows. Its huge iron doors were closed, but you could hear music coming from inside. I think they were singing, "How Sweet the Name of Jesus Sounds." I remembered reading about that song in history class—reading that John Newton was a slave ship captain when he wrote it.[1]

I pointed this out to Grandpa. He just smiled. He pointed to the gold letters that arched above the doorway of the church: DELIVERANCE.

"I don't know the answers," he said, "But the answers are in there."

Then, "Come on, boy," he whispered. "We'd better be getting you back on that M15 bus." And then Grandpa said something that I didn't quite understand. I'd never heard him talk like this before. He said, "The violence of the raging sun has melted into the cool night of indifference, and who knows what the morning will bring. You better get on home, now. It's almost midnight in the Promised Land."

Notes

Chapter 1: The Ancient Patriarch

[1]Cain Hope Felder, ed., *Stony the Road We Trod* (Philadelphia: Augsburg Fortress, 1991, p. 151.

[2]John Jackson, *Introduction to African Civilizations* (New York: Carol, 1970), p. 153.

[3]G. Mohktar, ed., *UNESCO General History of Africa*, vol. 2 (Berkeley: University of Californial Press, 1981), p. 41.

[4]Ibid., p. 43.

[5]Basil Davidson, *African Civilization Revisited* (Trenton, N.J.: World, 1993), p. 64.

[6]Ibid., p. 61.

[7]Alfred G. Dunston, *The Black Man in the Old Testament & Its World* (Philadelphia: Dorrance, 1974), p. 37.

[8]Richard Poe, *Black Spark, White Fire* (New York: Prima, 1997), pp. 25-26.

[9]John Taylor, *Egypt and Nubia* (Cambridge, Mass.: Harvard University Press, 1991), p. 5.

[10]Ibid.

[11]Felder, *Stony the Road We Trod*, p. 152.

[12]Ibid.

[13]Cain Hope Felder, ed., *Troubling Biblical Waters* (Maryknoll, N.Y.: Orbis, 1989), pp. 32-33.

[14]Charles B. Copher, *Black Biblical Studies: An Anthology of Charles B. Copher* (Chicago: Black Light Fellowship, 1993), p. 64.

[15]J. Daniel Hays, "From the Land of the Bow: Black Soldiers in the Ancient Near East," *Bible Review* (August 1998), p. 32.

[16]Copher, *Black Biblical Studies*, pp. 25-30.

[17]David Tuesday Adamo, *Africa & the Africans* (San Francisco: Christian University Press, 1998), p. 12.

[18]Ibid.

[19]St. Clair Drake, *Black Folk Here & There* (Los Angeles: Center for Afro-American Studies, University of California, 1987), p. 241.

[20]Mohktar, *UNESCO General History of Africa*, p. 287.

[21]William Y. Adams, *Corridor to Africa* (Princeton, N.J.: Princeton University Press, 1997), p. 264.

[22]Molefi Asante, *Classical Africa* (Maywood, N.J.: People's Publishing Group, 1994), p. 67.

[23]Frank M. Snowden Jr., *Blacks in Antiquity* (Cambridge, Mass.: Belknap, 1970), p. 114.

[24]Adams, *Corridor to Africa*, p. 267.

[25]Quoted in Jackson, *Introduction to African Civilizations*, p. 115.

[26]J. E. Manchip White, *Ancient Egypt: Its Culture & History* (New York: Dover, 1970), p. 189.

[27]Ibid., p. 190.

[28]Ibid., p. 94.

[29]Snowden, *Blacks in Antiquity,* p. 115.

[30]Ibid., p. 122.

[31]Ibid., p. 123.

[32]Ibid., pp. 130-31.

[33]Hays, "From the Land of the Bow," pp. 29-50.

[34]Walter Arthur McCray, *The Black Presence in the Bible,* vol. 2: *The Table of Nations, Genesis 10:1-32* (Chicago: Black Light Fellowship, 1990), pp. 126-27.

[35]William Moseley, *What Color Was Jesus?* (Chicago: African American Images, 1987), p. 7.

Chapter 2: Black West Africa

[1]Quoted in John G. Jackson, *Introduction to African Civilizations* (New York: Carol, 1970), p. 20.

[2]J. C. deGraft-Johnson, *African Glory* (Baltimore: Black Classics, 1986), p. 88.

[3]Maulana Karenga, *Introduction to Black Studies* (Los Angeles: University of Sankore Press, 1993), p. 90.

[4]deGraft-Johnson, *African Glory,* p. 82.

[5]Jackson, *Introduction to African Civilizations,* p. 81.

[6]Basil Davidson, *African Civilization Revisited* (Trenton, N.J.: African World Press, 1993), pp. 86-87.

[7]Karenga, *Introduction to Black Studies,* pp. 91-92.

[8]deGraft-Johnson, *African Glory,* p. 81.

[9]Ibid., p. 96.

[10]Karenga, *Introduction to Black Studies,* p. 93.

[11]R. Maw El Fasi, ed., *UNESCO General History of Africa,* vol. 3 (Berkeley: University of California Press, 1981), p. 151.

[12]J. Fade Ajayi and Michael Crowder, *History of West Africa,* vol. 1 (London: Longman, 1976), p. 127.

[13]Florence T. Polatnick and Alberta L. Saletan, *Shapers of Africa* (New York: Julia Mesner, 1969), p. 23.

[14]El Fasi, *UNESCO General History of Africa,* p. 149.

[15]K. B. C. Onwubiko, *School Certificate History of West Africa A. D. 1000-1800,* bk. 1 (Nigeria, West Africa: African-FEP Publishing, 1982), p. 39.

[16]Polatnick and Saletan, *Shapers of Africa,* p. 29.

[17]Jackson, *Introduction to African Civilizations,* p. 210.

[18]D. T. Niane, ed., UNESCO General History of Africa, vol. 4 (Berkeley: University of California Press, 1981), p. 197.

[19]Ibid., p. 200.

[20]Jackson, *Introduction to African Civilizations,* p. 217.

Chapter 3: Slavemakers

[1]J. C. deGraft-Johnson, *African Glory* (Baltimore: Black Classics, 1968), p. 127.

[2]Richard Oaniyan, ed., *African History & Culture* (Ikeja, Lagos, Nigeria: Longman, 1982), p. 62.

[3]Daniel P. Mannix and Malcolm Cowley, *Black Cargoes* (New York: Viking, 1962), p. 34.

[4]Douglas Grant, *The Fortunate Slave: An Illustration of African Slavery in the Early Eighteenth Century* (New York: Oxford University Press, 1968), p. 52.

[5]Basil Davidson, *The African Slave Trade* (Boston: Little, Brown, 1980), p. 28.

[6]Florent T. Polatnick and Alberta L. Saletan, *Shapers of Africa* (New York: Julia Messner, 1969), p. 48.

[7]Milton Metzer, ed., *In Their Own Words* (New York: Thomas Y. Cromwell, 1964), p. 67.

[8]James Walvin, *Slavery & the Slave Trade: A Short Illustrated History* (Jackson: University Press of Mississippi, 1983), p. 58.

[9]Davidson, *African Slave Trade,* p. 67.

[10]Ibid., p. 102.

[11]Mannix and Cowley, *Black Cargoes,* p. 22.

[12]Polatnick and Saletan, *Shapers of Africa,* p. 74.

[13]Davidson, *The African Slave Trade,* p. 242.

[14]Ibid., p. 251.

[15]Maulana Karenga, *Introduction to Black Studies* (Los Angeles: University of Sankore Press, 1993), p. 119.

[16]John Hope Franklin, *From Slavery to Freedom* (New York: Alfred A. Knopf, 1980), p. 44.

[17]Walvin, *Slavery & the Slave Trade,* p. 107.

Chapter 4: Slavery in the United States of America

[1]John R. Aldren, *George Washington: A Biography* (Baton Rouge: Louisiana State University, 1984), p. 212.

[2]Fritz Hirschfeld, *George Washington & Slavery* (St. Louis: University of Missouri Press, 1997), p. 74.

[3]Nathaniel Weyl and William Marina, *American Statesmen on Slavery & the Negro* (New Rochelle, N.Y.: Arlington House, 1971), p. 30.

[4]Joseph J. Ellis, *American Sphinx: The Character of Thomas Jefferson* (New York: Alfred A. Knopf, 1997), p. 144.

[5]Ibid., p. 149.

[6]David Brion Davis, *The Problem of Slavery in the Age of Revolution, 1770-1823* (Ithaca, N.Y.: Cornell University Press, 1975), p. 196.

[7]Carter G. Woodson and Charles Wesley, *The Negro in Our History* (Washington, D.C.: Associated Publishers, 1966), p. 28.

[8]Janet Duitsman Cornelius, *When I Can Read My Title Clear* (Columbia: University of South Carolina Press, 1991), p. 66.

[9]Ibid.

Chapter 5: Plantation Life

[1]Quoted in Willie Lee Rose, *A Documentary History of Slavery in North America* (New York: Oxford University Press, 1976), pp. 157-58.

[2]Stephen Oates, *The Fires of Jubilee* (New York: Mentor, 1975), p. 33.

[3]Philip Foner, *History of Black Americans* (Westport, Conn.: Greenwood, 1983), p. 57.

[4]Ibid.

[5]Quoted in James Blassingame, *The Slave Community* (New York: Oxford University Press, 1974), p. 234.

[6]Quoted in Blassingame, *Slave Community,* p. 234.

[7]Booker T. Washington, *Up From Slavery* (New York: Gramercy, 1993), p. 4.

[8]James Mellon, *Bullwhip Days* (New York: Widefeld & Nicholson, 1978), p. 43.

[9]Paul D. Escott, *Slavery Remembered* (Chapel Hill: University of North Carolina

Press, 1979), p. 46.

[10]Foner, *History of Black Americans,* p. 52.

[11]Mellon, *Bullwhip Days,* p. 48.

[12]Fritz Hirshfeld, *George Washington and Slavery,* (St. Louis: University of Missouri, 1997), p. 24.

[13]Frederick Douglass, *My Bondage & My Freedom* (Chicago: Johnson, 1990), p. 226.

[14]Anita Hill, *Quotations in Black* (Westport, Conn.: Greenwood, 1981), p. 41.

[15]Nathaniel Weyl and William Marina, *American Statesmen on Slavery & the Negro* (New Rochelle, N.Y.: Arlington House, 1971), p. 40.

[16]Eli Ginzberg and Alfred Eichner, *The Troublesome Presence* (London: Free Press of Glencoe, 1964), p. 153.

[17]Ibid., 154.

Chapter 6: Roots of the Black Church

[1]J. C. deGraft-Johnson, *African Glory* (Baltimore: Black Classics, 1986), p. 132.

[2]Ibid., p. 133.

[3]Ibid., p. 136.

[4]Ibid., p. 137.

[5]Carter G. Woodson, *The History of the Negro Church* (Washington, D.C.: Associated Publishers, 1972), p. 5-19.

[6]Albert Raboteau, *Slave Religion* (New York: Oxford University Press, 1978), p. 213.

[7]Ibid., p. 68.

[8]Ibid.

[9]Ibid., p. 307.

[10]Gayraud S. Wilmore, *Black Religion & Black Radicalism* (Maryknoll, N.Y.: Orbis, 1986), p. 54.

[11]Ibid.

[12]Ibid., p. 57-62.

[13]Eli Ginzberg and Alfred Eichner, *The Troublesome Presence* (London: Free Press of Glencoe, 1964), p. 120.

[14]Benjamin Elijah Mays and Joseph William Nicholson, *The Negro Church* (New York: Arno Press, 1969), p. 38.

[15]Ibid., p. 42.

[16]Mays and Nicholson, *Negro Church,* p. 22.

[17]Ibid.

[18]Quoted in C. Eric Lincoln and Lawrence H. Mamiya, *The Black Church in the African-American Experience* (Durham, N.C.: Duke University Press, 1990), p. 51.

[19]John Boles, *Masters & Slaves in the House of the Lord* (Lexington: University Press of Kentucky, 1988), p. 24.

[20]Quoted in Boles, *Masters & Slaves,* p. 33.

[21]Jean R. Sonderland, *Quakers & Slavery* (Princeton, N.J.: Princeton University Press, 1985), p. 76.

[22]David Chesbrough, *Clergy & Dissent in the Old South, 1830-1865* (Carbondale: Southern Illinois University Press, 1996), p. 13.

[23]James Gillespie Birney, *The American Churches: The Bulwarks of American Slavery* (New York: Arno, 1969), p. 8.

[24]Ibid.

[25]*National Anti-Slavery Standard* 23, no. 34 (January 1963): n.p.

[26]Ibid.

[27]Ernest Crosby, *Garrison: The Non-Resistant* (Chicago: Public Publishing, 1972), pp. 9-10.

[28]Quoted in Crosby, *Garrison,* p. 32.

[29]Ibid., pp. 25-32.

[30]Quoted in Jules Archer, *Angry Abolitionist: William Lloyd Garrison* (New York: Julia Messner, 1969), p. 110.

[31]Quoted in William S. McFeeley, *Frederick Douglass* (New York: William Norton, 1991), p. 30.

[32]Frederick Douglass, *Narrative of the Life of Frederick Douglass, An American Slave* (New York: Penguin, 1986), p. 112.

[33]Ibid., p. 133.

[34]Quoted in David Walker, *David Walker Appeal* (Baltimore: Black Classics, 1993), p. 63.

[35]Paul Finkelman, *His Soul Goes Marching On* (Charlottesville: University of Virginia Press, 1995), pp. 94-95.

[36]Ibid., p. 95.

[37]Ibid., p. 24.

[38]Ibid., p. 95.

[39]Ibid., p, 149.

[40]Stephen B. Oates, *I, John Brown* (New York: Harper & Row, 1970), p. 341.

[41]Ibid., p. 359.

[42]Charles Nichols, *Many 1000s Gone* (Leiden: E. J. Brill, 1963), pp. 22-23.

[43]Milton Meltzer, ed., *In Their Own Words* (New York: Thomas Y. Cromwell, 1964), p. 7.

Chapter 7: Civil War Divides the Union

[1]Quoted in Mark E. Neely Jr., *The Last Best Hope on Earth* (Cambridge, Mass.: Presidents and Fellows of Harvard University, 1993), p. 197.

[2]Ibid., p. 3.

[3]Quoted in Neely, *Last Bast Hope on Earth,* p. 111.

[4]Quoted in Eli Ginzberg and Alfred Eichern, *The Troublesome Presence* (London: Free Press of Glencoe, 1964), p. 116.

[5]"Freedom in the Abstract," *National Anti-Slavery Standard* 23, no. 33 (December 1962) p. 27.

[6]Neeley, *The Last Best Hope on Earth,* p. 98.

[7]Quoted in James M. McPherson, *The Struggle for Equality* (Princeton, N.J.: Princeton University Press, 1995), p. 116.

[8]Quoted in McPherson, *Struggle for Equality,* p. 193.

[9]Quoted in McPherson, *Struggle for Equality,* pp. 206-7.

[10]Quoted in McPherson, *Struggle for Equality,* p. 193.

[11]Ibid., p. 169.

[12]Arna Bontemps, *100 Years of Negro Freedom* (New York: Dodd, Mead, 1961), pp. 2-3.

[13]Ibid.

[14]Quoted in Neeley, *The Last Best Hope on Earth,* p. 120.

[15]Joel Williamson, *The Negro in South Carolina During Reconstruction, 1861-1877* (Hanover, N.H.: University Press of New England, 1990), p. 35.

[16]Ibid., p. 39.

[17]Paul D. Escott, *Slavery Remembered* (Chapel Hill: University of North Carolina Press, 1979), p. 134.

Chapter 8: Reconstruction
[1]Eric Foner, *America's Unfinished Revolution* (New York: Harper & Row, 1988), p. 4.
[2]Ibid., p. 9.
[3]Ibid., p. 10.
[4]Patrick W. Riddleberger, *1866: The Critical Year Revisited* (Carbondale: Southern Illinois University Press, 1979), p. 66.
[5]Ibid.
[6]Quoted in Arna Bontemps, *100 Years of Negro Freedom* (New York: Dodd, Mead, 1961), p. 16.
[7]W. E. B. DuBois, *Black Reconstruction* (New York: Russell & Russell, 1962), p. 341.
[8]Quoted in Stetson Kennedy, *After Appomattox* (Gainesville: University Press of Florida, 1995), p. 53.
[9]E. Franklin Frazier, *The Negro in the United States* (New York: Macmillan, 1957), p. 128.
[10]John Hope Franklin, *Reconstruction After the Civil War* (Chicago: University of Chicago Press, 1994), p. 48.
[11]Peter Kolchin, *The Responses of Alabama's Blacks to Emancipation and Reconstruction* (Westport, Conn.: Greenwood, 1992), pp. 120-21.
[12]Kennedy, *After Appomattox,* p. 114.

Chapter 9: The Rise of the New African-American Leaders
[1]C. Vann Woodward, *The Strange Career of Jim Crow* (New York: Oxford University Press, 1974), p. 71.
[2]James Michael Brodie, *The Lives and Ideas of America's Great Innovators* (New York: William Morrow, 1993), p. 54.
[3]Ibid., p. 94.
[4]Alfreda M. Duster, ed., *Crusade for Justice: The Autobiography of Ida B. Wells* (Chicago: University of Chicago Press), p. 18.
[5]Ibid., p. 19.
[6]Ibid., p. 66.
[7]Rachan Holt, *Mary McLeod Bethune: A Biography* (Garden City, N.J.: Doubleday, 1964), p. 59.
[8]Ibid.
[9]Ibid., p. 122.
[10]Booker T. Washington, *Up From Slavery* (Avenel, N.J.: Gramercy, 1993), p. 35.
[11]Ibid., p. 39.
[12]Gary R. Kremer, ed., *George Washington Carver: In His Own Words* (Columbia: University of Missouri Press, 1987), pp. 102-10.
[13]Washington, *Up From Slavery,* p. 161.
[14]W. E. B. DuBois, *The Souls of Black Folk* (Chicago: A. C. McClurg, 1903), p. 41.
[15]Ibid., p. 51.
[16]Ibid., p. 14.
[17]W. E. B. DuBois, *Dark Waters* (New York: A.M.S. Press, 1964), p. 27.
[18]DuBois, *The Souls of Black Folk,* p. 14.
[19]Walter White, *A Man Called White* (New York: Arno, 1969), p. 3.

[20]Ibid., p. 51.

[21]Charles E. Silberman, *Crisis in Black & White* (New York: Vintage, 1964), pp. 25-42.

[22]Jay David and Elaine Crane, eds., *The Black Soldier* (New York: Praeger, 1971), pp. 109-30.

[23]Philip S. Foner, *Blacks in the Military in American History* (New York: Praeger, 1974), p. 114.

[24]Jervis Anderson, *A. Philip Randolph: A Biographical Portrait* (New York: Harcourt Brace Jovanovich, 1973), p. 225.

[25]Rupert Lewis, *Marcus Garvey: Anti-Colonial Champion* (Trenton, N.J.: African World, 1988), p. 77.

[26]E. David Cronon, *Black Moses: The Story of Marcus Garvey and the Universal Negro Improvement Association* (Madison: University of Wisconsin Press, 1974), p. 45.

[27]Ibid.

[28]Ibid., p. 79.

[29]Judith Stein, *The World of Marcus Garvey* (Baton Rouge: Louisiana State University Press, 1986), p. 154.

[30]Anderson, *A. Philip Randolph,* p. 131.

[31]Quoted in Anderson, *A. Philip Randolph,* p. 131.

[32]Elton G. Fox, *The Story of a Pioneer Black Nationalist* (New York: Dodd, Mead, 1972), p. 169.

[33]Quoted in Cronon, *Black Moses,* p. 137.

Chapter 10: The Civil Rights Movement

[1]Taylor Branch, *Parting the Waters* (New York: Simon & Schuster, 1988), p. 135.

[2]Ibid., pp. 136-37.

[3]Quoted in Branch, *Parting the Waters,* p. 140.

[4]Ibid., p. 141.

[5]Branch, *Parting the Waters,* p. 193.

[6]Ibid., p. 97.

[7]Ibid., p. 100.

[8]Quoted in Branch, *Parting the Waters,* p. 109.

[9]Branch, *Parting the Waters,* p. 106.

[10]Ibid., p. 118.

[11]August Meier and Elliot Richard, *CORE: A Study in the Civil Rights Movement* (New York: Oxford University Press, 1973), p. 136.

[12]Branch, *Parting the Waters,* p. 425.

[13]Howell Raines, *My Soul Is Rested* (New York: Putnam's, 1977), p. 107.

[14]Henry Hampton, Steven Fayer, Sarah Flynn and Barbara Rich, *Voices of Freedom* (New York: Bantam, 1990), p. 23.

[15]Quoted in Raines, *My Soul Is Rested.*

[16]Quoted in James Washington, ed., *Testament of Hope,* (San Francisco: Harper Collins, 1990), pp. 284-302.

[17]Branch, *Parting the Waters,* p. 881.

Chapter 11: The Rise, Fall & Rise of Malcolm X

[1]Peter Goldman, *The Death & Life of Malcolm X* (Urbana: University of Illinois, 1979), p. 27.

[2]Malcolm X with Alex Haley, *Autobiography of Malcolm X* (New York, Grove, 1965), p. 3.

[3]Ibid., p. 38.

[4]Ibid., p. 32.

[5]Ibid., pp. 35-36.

[6] Quoted in David Gallen, *Malcolm X As They Knew Him* (New York: Carroll & Graf, 1992), p. 113.

[7]Ibid., pp. 12-13.

[8]Benjamin Karim with Peter Skutches and David Gallen, *Remembering Malcolm* (New York: Pathfinder, 1989), p. 125.

[9]Goldman, *Death and Life of Malcolm X,* p. 118.

[10]Quoted in Goldman, *Death and Life of Malcolm X,* p. 119.

Chapter 12: The Changing of the Guard

[1]Martin Luther King Jr., *Where Do We Go from Here: Chaos or Community?* (New York: Harper & Row, 1968), p. 133.

[2]James Cone, *Martin & Malcolm & America* (Maryknoll, N.Y.: Orbis, 1991), p. 222.

[3]Quoted in *Martin & Malcolm & America,* p. 222.

[4]Ralph David Abernathy, *And the Walls Came Tumbling Down* (New York: Harper-Perennial, 1989), p. 363.

[5]Ibid., pp. 370-71.

[6]Ibid., p. 376.

[7]Quoted in Louis Lomax, *To Kill a Black Man* (Los Angeles: Holloway House, 1987), p. 167.

[8]Lomax, *To Kill a Black Man,* p. 167.

Chapter 13: America in Flames

[1]" 'Newark Race Riot: Open Rebellion Just Like in War Time,' " *U. S. News & World Report* (July 24, 1967), p. 6.

[2]"The Real Tragedy of Newark," *U. S. News & World Report* (July 31, 1967), p. 30.

[3]Ibid., p. 37.

[4]Ibid.

[5]Quoted in "Races," *Time* (July 28, 1967).

[6]Quoted in *Time* (August 4, 1967), p. 16.

[7]H. Rap Brown, *Die Nigger Die: A Political Biography* (New York: Dial, 1969), p. 2.

[8]Ibid.

[9]Ibid.

[10]Quoted in "Black Militants Talk of Guns and Guerillas," *Time* (August 4, 1967), p. 17.

[11]Quoted in "Black Militants Talk," p. 17.

[12]"Black Militants Talk," p. 17.

[13]Quoted in "LBJ's Ideas on How to Stop Riots in the Nation's Cities," *U. S. News & World Report* (August 7, 1967), pp. 56-57.

[14]Quoted in "How to Start a Riot," *U. S. News & World Report* (August 21, 1967), p. 8.

[15]"Memphis: An Ugly Portent," *Newsweek* (April 3, 1968), p. 33.

[16]Quoted in *Newsweek* (April 15, 1968), p. 35.

[17]David J. Garrow, *Bearing the Cross* (New York: William Morrow, 1986), p. 622.

[18]Quoted in *U. S. News & World Report* (April 22, 1968), p. 27.

[19]Quoted in *U. S. News & World Report* (June 3, 1968), p. 48.

[20]Ibid., p. 47.

[21]Ralph David Abernathy, *And the Walls Came Tumbling Down* (New York: HarperPerennial, 1989), p. 528.

[22]Quoted in David Hilliard and Lewis Cole, *This Side of Glory* (Boston: Little, Brown, 1993), p. 115.

[23]*Report of the National Advisory Commission on Civil Disorders* (New York: Bantam, 1968), p. 2.

[24]Quoted in Bobby Seale, *Seize the Time* (Baltimore: Black Classics, 1991), p. 52.

[25]Huey P. Newton, *Revolutionary Suicide* (New York: Harcourt Brace Jovanovich, 1973), p. 1.

[26]Ibid., p. 131.

[27]Quoted in Black Panther flier, courtesy of the Blockson Collection, Temple University, Philadelphia, n.d.

[28]Philip S. Foner, ed., *The Black Panthers Speak* (New York: De Capo, 1995), p. 19.

[29]David Garrow, *The F.B.I. & Martin Luther King Jr.* (New York: William Norton, 1981), p. 49.

[30]Ibid., p. 102.

[31]Ibid., p. 49.

[32]Karl Evanzz, *Judas Factor* (New York: Thunder's Mouth, 1992), p. 246.

[33]Ibid., p. 294.

[34]Kenneth O'Reilly, *Racial Matters: The FBI's Secret File on Black America 1960-1972* (New York: Free Press, 1991), pp. 305-20.

Chapter 14: Black Money

[1]Andrew Hacker, *Two Nations: Black and White, Separate, Hostile, Unequal* (New York: Ballantine, 1995), pp. 3-4.

[2]Cornel West, *Race Matters* (New York: Vintage, 1994), pp. 3-4.

[3]Farai Chideya, *Don't Believe the Hype* (New York: Plume, 1995), pp. 117, 120-21.

[4]Ibid., p. 122.

[5]Ibid., p. 47.

[6]"The State of Black America," National Urban League (1998), p. 17.

[7]Chideya, *Don't Believe the Hype,* p. 49.

[8]Richard J. Herrenstein and Charles Murray, *The Bell Curve* (New York: Simon & Schuster, 1995), p. 340.

[9]Ibid., p. 312.

[10]Chideya, *Don't Believe the Hype,* pp. 244-45.

[11]Kristina Shevory, "Anti-209 Groups Hold Massive March," *Daily Californian* (Berkeley), (August 29, 1997), p. 1.

[12]Quoted in *Emerge* (March 1996), p. 40.

[13]Ibid.

[14]Ibid., p. 42.

[15]Shelby Steele, *The Content of Our Character* (New York: St. Martin's, 1990), p. 21.

[16]Ibid., p. 23.

[17]*San Francisco Focus,* p. 61.

[18]Ibid.

[19]Quoted in *San Francisco Focus,* p. 124.

[20]Quoted in Kathy Chu, "Initiative Promises a Photo-Finish," *Daily Californian* (Berkeley), (November 1, 1996), p. 3.

[21]*San Francisco Focus,* p. 125.

[22]Claud Anderson, *Black Labor, White Wealth* (Edgewood, Md.: Duncan & Duncan, 1994), pp. 16-17.

[23]Quoted in Roger D. Katz, ed., *Straight from the Heart* (Philadelphia: Fortress Press, 1981), p. 20.

Chapter 15: African-American in the Inner City
[1]Derek Walters, interview by author, Hillside, N.J., fall 1995.

[2]"State of Black America Report," National Urban League (1998), p. 112.

[3]"Caged Cargo," *Emerge* (October 1997), p. 38.

[4]Nancy R. Gibbs, "Murder in Miniature," *Time* (September 19, 1994), pp. 58-59.

[5]Nelson George, ed., *Stop the Violence* (New York: Pantheon, 1987), p. 47.

[6]Ibid., p. 66.

[7]Peter Applebone, "Report: Minorities Slipping Behind," *San Francisco Examiner* (December 29, 1996), p. 6.

[8]William Julius Wilson, *When Work Disappears* (New York: Alfred A. Knopf, 1996), pp. 29, 30.

[9]Quoted in Sylvester Monroe, "America's Most Feared," *Emerge* (October 1995), p. 27.

[10]William H. Grier and Price M. Cobbs, *Black Rage* (New York: Basic Books, 1968), p. 60.

[11]Mike McClary, *Cop Shot: The Murder of Ed Byrne* (New York: Putnam's, 1990), p. 23.

[12]"State of Black America," p. 286.

[13]Carol Adams and Scott Minerbrook, "Lives Without Fathers," *U. S. & World News Report* (February 27, 1995), p. 52.

[14]Ibid.

[15]Quoted in John Leland and Allison Samuels, "The New Generation Gap," *Newsweek* (March 17, 1997), p. 55.

[16]Denene Miller, Chrisena Coleman, Helen Kennedy and Dan Whitcomb, "Whosoever Believeth," *New York Daily News,* March 10, 1997, p. 5.

[17]Toure Muhammad, "Hip Hop Summit," *Final Call* (April 15, 1997), p. 10.

Chapter 16: The Second Resurrection
[1]Quoted in Louis Lomax, *When the Word Is Given* (Cleveland: World, 1963), pp. 113-14.

[2]Ibid., p. 114.

[3]Quoted in C. Eric Lincoln, *The Black Muslims in America* (Queens, N.Y.: Kayode, 1973), p. 78.

[4]Lincoln, *Black Muslims,* p. 29

[5]Ibid., p. 81.

[6]Quoted in Arthur J. Magida, *Prophet of Rage* (New York: BasicBooks, 1996), p. 32.

[7]Quoted in Ted Stewart, "Who Will Inherit the $80 Million Black Muslim Empire?"

[8]Steven Barboza, "A Divided Legacy," *Emerge* (April 1992), p. 27.

[9]Ibid.

[10]Wallace Deen Muhammad, *As the Light Shineth from the East* (Chicago: WDM Publishing, 1980), p. 11.

[11]Barboza, *American Jihad,* p. 99.

[12]Quoted in Arthur J. Magida, *A Prophet of Rage* (New York: BasicBooks, 1996), p. 118.

[13]Quoted in Magida, *Prophet of Rage,* p. 122.

[14]William A. Henry III, "Pride and Prejudice," *Time* (May 28, 1994), p. 26.

[15]Ibid., p. 25.

[16]Barboza, *American Jihad,* p. 99.

[17]Henry, "Pride and Prejudice," p. 23.

[18]"Time's 25 Most Influential Americans," *Time* (June 17, 1996), p. 67.

[19]James Muhammad and Askia Muhammad, "Minister Farrakhan's World Friendship Tour," *Final Call* (February 14, 1996).

[20]John Leland and Allison Samuels, "The New Generation Gap," *Newsweek* (March 17, 1997) p. 27.

[21]*New York Amsterdam News* (October 1996), p. 1.

[22]"John F. Kennedy Jr.: One in a Million", *George* (October 1997), p. 109.

[23]Vern Smith, "My Duty Is to Point Out the Wrong and the Evil," *Newsweek* (October 30, 1995).

Chapter 17: The Rise of the New Black Church

[1]J. Alfred Smith, interview with author, Berkeley, Calif., fall 1997.

[2]J. Alfred Smith, *Falling in Love with God* (Chicago: Urbana Ministries, 1997), p. 103.

Epilogue

[1]Hugh Thomas, *The Slave Trade: The Story of the Atlantic Slave Trade 1440-1870* (New York: Simon & Schuster, 1997), p. 309.

Index